THE BRANDFUL WORKFORCE

How Employees Can <u>Make</u>, Not Break Your Brand

JULIA GOMETZ

Glastonbury Press
The Brandful Workforce – How Employees Can Make, Not Break
Your Brand
Julia Gometz

Design and Interior Images: Alison Crawford
Video Book Trailer: Catharine Fennell and Todd Smith
Brandfulworkforce.com Website: Fred Tatlyan

Published in the United States by Glastonbury Press
ISBN: 0989815900
ISBN 13: 9780989815901

When the magic of the brand is truly felt by the workforce, it can be called brandful.

To my husband, Alex
and my children, Emma, Leah, Owen and Ella

CONTENTS

INTRODUCTION
It's a Win-Win

Birth of the Idea 1
Setting Your Expectations 7
My Philosophy 11

ONE
How to Build a Brandful Workforce in Your Organization

The Brandful Workforce Road Map 15
What Is It All About? 15
Pre-Requisites 23
The Road Map Unveiled 25

TWO
How to Build a Business Employees Want to Promote

Brandful Business Basics 29
Your Business Model 31
Business Model Checklist 42
Your Customer Promise 45
Customer Promise Checklist 54

Your Employee Promise 57
Employee Promise Checklist 76

THREE

How to Involve Employees in Your Brand

The Six Brandful Channels 83
Channel #1 – Communication 85
Channel #2 – Citizenship 97
Channel #3 – Employee Programs 105
Channel #4 – Celebration 113
Channel #5 – Swag 121
Channel #6 – Recruitment 127

FOUR

How to Hire Brandful Employees

The Brand GAP in Recruiting 133
The Six Obstacles to Brandful Recruiting 137
How to Attract and Hire Brandful Employees 141
Take The Brand Gap Challenge 151

FIVE

How to Become Brandful Individually

Becoming Brandful 153
Your Brand Profile: Who Are You? 159
Finding Your Match 163
How to Be Brandful 167

Q & A WITH MY READERS

ACKNOWLEDGMENTS

THE BRANDFUL WORKFORCE

How Employees Can <u>Make</u>,
Not Break Your Brand

FOLLOW THE DISCUSSION ONLINE
HTTP://BRANDFULWORKFORCE.COM/BOOK

INTRODUCTION

It's a Win-Win

Birth of the Idea

Entering the job market at seventeen was a time that I first think of myself as being brandful—even though that term didn't yet exist. I was told by the "higher-ups"—aka my parents—to go out and look for a summer job. It was springtime, and all my friends went to the closest store or the first place they could think of to apply for minimum wage. My identical twin sister and I had made a pact to never—not ever—go out and do what everybody else does. So when it came to a job, we not only wanted to be different, we wanted a job we could be excited about. We thought about our dream job and what our passions were, which at that time were the same. We loved travel. We were friendly and chatty girls who loved meeting new people, and got the idea to work in a hotel, possibly at the front desk.

Instead of looking in the classifieds, we started our first job search completely out of the box, by searching out our favorite hotels in downtown Ottawa, Canada's capital, where we would be "head over heels" to work. We started with the fanciest, of course. Why not? (Lesson Number One: Dream Big. Go for the gold. It doesn't hurt to try.) We went to the Chateau Laurier—even the name sounds grand. It was a huge chateau-like hotel, right next to the Parliament buildings. We started out unannounced and simply asked for the head of human resources at the front desk. We dropped off our résumés, after being told nobody was available to meet with us without an appointment. How dare they? Wouldn't any employer be eager to meet us, let alone hire us?

We were disappointed at first that there were no bites. We finally got a callback after the third or fourth hotel—a beautiful downtown hotel with the only revolving restaurant in town and a grand lobby. I remember meeting with the vice president of human resources, who asked me what I was looking for. The question itself—*What are you looking for?*—sent me into a dream state. I could feel my eyes light up with excitement as I could envision my dream first summer job. I told him that I was a "people-person" and would love to greet hotel guests, answer questions, guide them around the city, and help them have fun. He said they were considering a new concierge service and asked if I would be up for it. In the end, he decided to hire both me and my identical twin sister for the same job. I would work 8:00 a.m. to 2:00 p.m. and she would work 2:00 p.m. to 8:00 p.m. It was the perfect scenario. Guests used to tell us, *Boy, you work a long day!* They didn't realize there were two of us.

Unbeknownst to me at the time, I was acting like a brandful employee, someone on the lookout for an organization whose service I wanted to promote. So, even though I only recently came up with the term "brandful," I feel like it has always been a part of me and who I am.

Professionally, the idea of a brandful workforce first came to me several years ago when I was working as a manager in the human resources department. I was asked to attend a marketing meeting with our business partner. I showed up in midtown Manhattan, excited to have been included in a cross-functional meeting. At the time, I was the senior advisor on the pulse of the employees. What are they thinking? What do they like or dislike about the company? At what level are they involved? What do they think of this idea or that idea? What are their pain points, their needs? I enjoyed my role very much, and had secretly taken a liking to marketing. I had seen firsthand how the employees prided themselves on the company's service and success. In fact, some employees named their top motivators as the customers themselves. The founder of the company used to tell the employees that our competitors were jealous, as they couldn't figure out how he could attract the nice customers, while they had to deal with the jerks. What our competitors didn't realize was that we didn't attract the nice customers; we knew how to treat customers to bring out their best, so it just appeared that way.

Back to the marketing meeting. Just as in any meeting, I found myself sitting around a large table in a conference room in front of a PowerPoint presentation. The business partner explained the reason I was invited from human resources, was that they were doing something called "inside-out" marketing. This was described as a campaign that would originate from the employees and the culture of the company. The marketing folks had it all thought out: *Let's give video cameras to all the employees so they can film clips that will go viral. We'll explain the campaign and how they can get involved, and they will be able to be aligned internally with our marketing campaign.*

The idea from the get-go didn't sit right with me. If the marketing campaign was already completely thought out and they were going to involve the employees at the end, that didn't really seem to me to be meaningful involvement. What if the employees didn't even like the campaign? Would they want to create videos? From my perspective, I had seen so many employees who had fabulous and energetic ideas about marketing that they wanted to share. They wanted to participate in the *creation of the campaign*, not just the deployment.

At that moment, as I sat in the conference room, brandful workforce as a concept started to take shape in my mind, something that I would later set out to define for other organizations. I would embark on a quest to find out how organizations foster employees who promote the brand. I didn't realize that this had never been done before; surely there was someone who might have considered this. But I would soon find out that this was a gap that I would need to fill. I would soon embark on building the first-ever road map for organizations. I would soon discover that even organizations that had a brandful workforce didn't exactly know how they managed to build them. And they didn't necessarily build them on purpose. They happened upon it because of their philosophies, operating principles, and business plans.

And it didn't surprise me to find folks from across disciplines—advertising, marketing, innovation, social media, corporate communications, corporate strategy, corporate learning, customer experience, citizenship, human resources—drawn to my quest. With the rise in social media, individuals have increased power in every way imaginable—what new role do employees have? Businesses cannot continue to run without the participation of hundreds, thousands, and millions of individual voices. So why not make these voices count *for* your brand?

The final push for this book came during my most recent role at JetBlue Airways, an airline that was created to bring humanity back to air travel. The number-one question I was typically asked by colleagues at other organizations was how they too could build a workforce of brand ambassadors. Quickly, I found myself serving as an informal mentor to other executives. Soon the number of folks interested in this topic grew. And there really wasn't anywhere for executives to turn for help. I knew that I had to take the plunge to build it myself. And I thought about that pact my sister and I had made. Guess what? Everyone else wasn't already doing it.

Setting Your Expectations

This book is not typical. It's different in three ways.

First, it asks a unique question that has not been adequately answered: *How can I build a workforce of brand ambassadors?* Not only has this question been rarely addressed, I contend that there has not been any viable answer submitted. Why? Because employees have never really had a recognized role or impact on the brand... until now. Typically, employees are not seen for their positive potential they can contribute beyond the standard job description. Yes, they are there to get the job done; however, there is much more that they can contribute if given the chance. Instead of an expense—or even worse, as problems with needs—your people who have traditionally been separated from organizational success can now more fully participate and shape it. Throw away the idea that a few executives at the top are responsible for success. It's only in the last decade that leaders have commonly understood that employees can be the driving force for success. When executives see the connection between employee engagement and bottom-line profits, their ears perk up. And when they see the harm that disgruntled employees can do, such as the investment banker who left Goldman Sachs (and some estimate the cost as more than a billion dollars to the company), they start listening.

This book is also different because its goal is to involve readers, such as yourself, to participate in answering the question. It is not intended to be the "end-all-be-all." Quite the opposite. This book is meant to pull readers into the discussion interactively, to continue to build, share, and improve upon what's presented. As you flip through, please send your thoughts through the links set up in this book and be a part of it. If you are reading this in hard copy, you can enter the discussion at www.brandfulwork-force.com/book. To get the most out of this book, go online and access the links provided. The videos offer additional insight that complement the book.

A final way the book is unique: It is told with two perspectives in mind. Both tell the same story: The Brandful Workforce—employees who work *for* the brand, not against it. However, each vantage point has a slightly different perspective. One perspective, that of the employer, is looking to build a brandful workforce—employees who can truly promote the product or service and who can improve the competitive advantage over other similar organizations. The other perspective considers the employee who wants to enjoy a meaningful, successful career and be valued. Yes, I'll say it again: just as you the employer want to build it, employees yearn to be a real and genuine part of a valued workforce.

In order to build a brandful workforce, the employee perspective must be better understood in relation to your business. Just as I was excited to find a top-notch hotel in Ottawa, Canada, there are employees who are searching and wanting to be part of your organization—if you have a product or service that fulfills a real need or desire., or something they can connect to.

Why did I write this with more than one perspective in mind?

Like some of you, I have attended and spoken at my fair share of conferences. But one really stuck in my mind that hit home on the meaning and value of different perspectives. It was a conference in Las Vegas in which a former symphony orchestra conductor presented a unique program on leadership. Roger, the conductor, had a small orchestra with him whose members were dispersed among the audience. I was sitting next to a trumpet. Roger was simultaneously the conductor and the speaker of the program. He had each of the musicians introduce themselves to the folks around them. (There were maybe five or so participants to each musician.) He warmed everyone up by having the orchestra play a short melody, and the excitement began as we could actually feel what it was like to be in the middle of an orchestra. Roger proceeded with one bit of music at a time, to make various points about an individual's perspective and how each one was slightly different. But his main point was at the end, when he asked certain participants to describe what they heard from where they were sitting. They each described something different. Of course, sitting with the trumpet player made it harder for me to hear the other instruments. Then he asked someone to stand in the conductor's spot and see if it sounded different. And it did. Each musician had a critical piece to play, but they had to focus on their own perspective and understand it was different from others. Each member of the orchestra depended on the others and the conductor to be successful. No perspective was right or wrong. It was that they each had an important role and together they were one and united in delivering the most beautiful music possible.

It's the same when it comes to organizational success. When everyone works together, they achieve the unthinkable. Employees and employers need each other. The Brandful Workforce is a win-win.

My Philosophy

I have a certain approach that defines my own personal brand. You will see this reflected throughout the book as well as in me, once you get to know me. Below is my modus operandi, or way of operating.

Be helpful, not hurtful.

Executive coaches advise leaders to praise in public, scold in private—it's not just a good business practice. I will be providing many great examples of organizations who have brandful employees. It is equally important to show examples of what's *not* brandful; however, I have chosen not to call those organizations out by name. I don't believe the names are as helpful as the lessons that can be learned and applied, which is my focus. *This book is meant to be helpful, not hurtful.*

Be passionate and true to myself and my readers.

I have no other purpose for writing this book other than pure passion. Having been on both sides—an employee and a leader—I am convinced that everyone needs to hear the message of this book—and brandful is a win-win in terms of improving the success of organizations as well as the individual workers.

Be practical and actionable.

This is an innovative how-to book rather than a complicated or lengthy read. I value the limited time of readers, and my goal is to get the major points across as quickly and effectively as possible so readers can take action.

Drive common sense into common practice.

Some executives (not you, of course) are allowing complexity to overrun and convolute their businesses. The brandful workforce model presented here is not complicated to understand. It makes sense and it's simple. We need to revive commonsense leadership and maybe it will become common practice.

Embrace change and accept that it is constant.

Brands evolve. People evolve. Everything evolves. Be open and aware of how and when change happens, and embrace it.

Inspire not just for inspiration's sake, but for action.

I'm not just interested in inspiring my readers to think differently, but to act differently; try something new. Prepare yourself, open your mind, and explore new ways of looking at yourself, your organization, your role, other organizations, and new ways of doing things in the future.

Have fun.

If there's not an ounce of fun in it, I don't want it. There should be a little bit (or a lot) of fun in every business...otherwise, you're missing out!

Moving Forward Through the Book

The first part of this book (one, two and three) details the road map. It includes the unveiling of the road map (one), and a deep dive on how to build a brandful workforce in your organization (two and three). Then, the second part of the book shows you how to evolve your current workforce through brandful recruiting (four) and how to become brandful individually (five). While writing the book, many questions came up that do not necessarily fit neatly elsewhere. At the end, you will find a conversational dialogue that provides answers to some of the common questions.

ONE

How to Build a Brandful Workforce in Your Organization

The Brandful Workforce Road Map

What Is It All About?

This section presents a simple and commonsense road map that you can use either to create a brandful workforce *or* to evaluate a workforce to determine how far or close an organization is to having a brandful workforce. The model consists of two parts. First, the Brandful Business Basics—how can you expect your employees to be brandful if you don't have a great product or service? Moving beyond that, when you know you've got the basics covered, but employees are not actively promoting the brand, you need the second phase: Employee Action—how to get them actively involved in your brand.

The first phase, Brandful Business Basics, has three parts:

1. *having a profitable business model—how you make money over the long term and can stay in business,*

2. *having and executing a clear customer promise—what you deliver and how you deliver it, and*

3. *having and executing a clear employee promise—what you promise to give your employees and what you expect in return.*

After the basics are in place, meaning a company has all the ingredients for employees to be brandful, we can move to the second phase of the model, which involves employees in the brand. *It bears repeating*: just because a fantastic organization delivers on its promises doesn't necessarily mean that employees will take the step of actually promoting the company. Phase two is taking the extra steps to provide the resources, tools, and support for employees to work *for* the brand.

Before we get to the road map, let's address the question: What is a brandful workforce and what is it *not*?

OK—I admit it: I didn't actually create the concept; I just created the word, "brandful." The phrase I had heard before is "workforce of brand ambassadors." There is also "brand evangelist," "brand advocate," and there are probably other terms as well. Sometimes you get a better idea of what something is when you consider what it is *not*. Let's look first at what a brandful workforce is *not*.

Hopefully you've gathered that a brandful workforce is not "inside-out" marketing, which to me, seems more of a scheme than anything else. (I say this lovingly to my marketing buddies.) It seems that the goal of inside-out marketing is more around marketing—or selling something—rather than creating authenticity. It is the marketer's response to clients who want their campaigns to include the workforce, only they don't know how to do it. Something I've seen some marketers do is ask the workforce a series of questions so they can better understand what they feel differentiates their organization from others, and how they can be more involved in the brand. I see organizations relying on and using information collected by existing employees to determine their next steps. What's wrong with this approach is that an organization should not have employees *lead* their *internal* brand. Yes, it's important to get their involvement, perspective, and feedback; however, the brand should be guided by the business model. Secondly, there is no internal brand that's separate from the external brand. Those are my concerns with this approach.

What else is it not? It's not a "branded workforce" or "employee branding." This would be more along the lines of branding a workforce like *everyone that works at Apple is young, hip, and innovative.* Although that is part of the concept, it is not the entire thing. And it's not "employer branding," which is how you think of a certain organization as a place to work (i.e. flexible work schedules, career development opportunities, and benefits). Similar to inside-out marketing above, an organizational brand cannot be separated from its employer brand—which is what I find missing in employer branding work. Oftentimes these folks work in isolation, which is my main concern. They typically ask questions like: *What kind of workforce do you want to attract?* or *What kind of internal organization are you?* or *Who are you internally?* These are good questions and necessary to answer, however first you must start with your business—your product or service. Employee strategy must be anchored in the business and not operate as a departmental silo.

A brandful workforce is not just about employee engagement, although that is also part of it. So much has been written on the topic that it's hard to tell which book to read. The main problem with employee engagement work is that it is not a goal…it's a means to a goal. What is an engaged employee engaged to do? An employee may be engaged in his specific work, but not engaged in teamwork or collaboration. There are ongoing concerns with engagement—and I should know, having created and headed the employee engagement program at JetBlue—in that it's not well defined or related to the business.

So what *is* a brandful workforce?

Simply put, a brandful workforce is one that works *for* the brand, not against it. It is a goal and a desired end-state that makes sense.

I hate to be so blunt, but what is wrong with a picture of three obese gym instructors? Would you want to work out with these folks? What would you think of the gym if you saw these instructors? It's exactly the same thinking for any organization, employee, and customer interaction. People are part of the brand.

Here's another recent example. I went to a medical clinic for a routine procedure. While the receptionist was checking me in, I couldn't help but notice she was munching on something in her mouth. In the background, I could see an empty bag of Cheetos in the garbage can. I am punishing myself for not taking a picture of the scene as the Cheetos bag happened to be in a garbage can located directly underneath the sign of the medical clinic. I couldn't help but think how contradictory they were. Even though the receptionist is not the doctor treating me, I would like to think that the doctor would want someone healthy representing her at the front desk.

A brandful workforce is authenticity.

So much these days seems to be a scheme. Even things that seem so genuine sometimes end up being strategically planned with ulterior motives. According to some marketers, *it's all just a lie…just make it a good lie that folks want to believe.* Well, I'm throwing all of this in the garbage, and I'm saying: *why not just tell the truth, but make the truth good?* Hey, I had a pretty good upbringing, and one thing my parents taught me well is to tell the truth. One thing that nobody can take away from you is your word. Someone who is always honest can be trusted. Let's go back in time and think of Honest Abe. I think many of us have forgotten this very simple, yet important value.

When your organization is doing something that is needed or desired (which every organization should be doing), the marketing should just be spreading around the truth behind why it's needed. Volvo provides the safest vehicle on the road. FedEx provides guaranteed delivery. Gerber was the first prepared baby food, helping moms everywhere. These are not gimmicks or lies. And as these companies evolve along with the competition, they need to continually check in with the customers to understand the real and honest reasons why they continue to purchase their products or services, because that is what's sustaining their brand.

Just be yourself. That is a theme in this book. We're all savvy these days. We can tell a lie from the truth. When an organization has what it takes to be successful, it doesn't need to lie. It's when the chips are down and an organization is struggling, the fingers start pointing and instead of making the necessary fixes or admitting defeat, the lies begin to form. People pay whom they trust. That's why Tiffany's can sell a diamond for a lot more than a jeweler in New York's Diamond District can. Customers pay a premium to get their expectations met. That's why Starbucks can charge more as well. It's an experience and a product specifically that the customer wants and is willing to pay for. If it's not executed consistently, customers won't continue to come. It's not the lie they believe, it's the consistent experience, the promise, and the specific product or service they want.

A brandful workforce is the employee living and being the brand.

In order for employees to be brandful, they need to be in alignment with the brand. I had lunch with one of the chief officers at a Fortune 100 company one day and we discussed the brandful workforce concept. She said:

> *Julia, what you're talking about is real. Genuine. It's not just a scheme or trying to sell someone something. It makes sense. It's connecting what you want your brand to be with what it really and truly is. And nobody gets it or does it.*

But maybe it's not just about alignment, which is side-by-side. A brandful workforce *is* the brand. It's not that something turns on when employees get to work. Take Game Stop, for example. They hire folks who are game fanatics and know their stuff. It's not that they only love games when they go to work. They're the type of employees who, if they're late, were playing a game at home and lost track of time.

Why is the integration of brand and workforce so rare?

I was meeting with another executive colleague. I told him about my book and he said:

It's tricky attracting candidates, because you end up telling them more of who you want to be than who you really are as an organization. We're working on improving things and know where we want to be, but if we tell them who we really are, they might not want to work here.

Do you agree or disagree? Comment here or read other comments: (http://brandfulworkforce.com/book/general-discussion).

Here's my opinion. Excuse my Southern (and yes, I did live in the South): Honey, this mentality ain't gonna fly in the future. Organizations will need to unveil who they really are and their plans to improve. New hires into an organization will then be in a position to work *for* the evolving brand, instead of being tricked into a brand that never really existed.

A brandful workforce is a goal, not a means to a goal.

Many books talk about alignment as the central theme, but alignment is not a goal. Just like engagement, it's a means to an end. A brandful workforce is the end—the desired state. It's tangible. Nobody can argue that they don't want a brandful workforce (on top of productivity and results—not in place of it.) But folks can argue forever about whether they need an engaged workforce, a satisfied workforce, a mission, etc. All these things will come into focus when you see a brandful workforce as your goal.

Pre-requisites

Before we look at the road map, there are two must-haves, or pre-requisites, that are nonnegotiable: CEO buy-in and collaboration.

1- "It's A Given" (CEO buy-in)

Over the years working at a people-centric organization, I was asked by colleagues at nonprofits, for-profits, and large and small shops, *How do you build such a gung-ho workforce?* JetBlue, which had opened for business on February 11, 2000, had a mission: bringing humanity back to air travel. People had been part of the competitive advantage and business strategy from day one. When I would give presentations at conferences, one of my favorite frequently asked questions was: *How did you convince your CEO or executive leadership that people were important?* or *How did you get executive buy-in for your programs?* My response: *I didn't need to convince anyone. They already believed people were critical. If you have to work too hard to get the buy-in, go somewhere else.*

Executive buy-in should not be overlooked, as I see oftentimes that it is a leading blocker to building a brandful workforce. Executives shouldn't need convincing. If they don't intuitively *get* that people can promote and be part of their brand, you must consider how likely it is that they can or will be persuaded by anyone else. I hate to see folks be hard on themselves for not having the best "how to influence and persuade others" skills, but sometimes it may not be you. For some executives, this is a new concept and bucks the old-school way of managing by slave-driving versus leading with inspiration.

So I was lucky. I didn't ever have to get executive buy-in for one of the most critical requirements for building a brandful workforce.

2- Culture of Collaboration—Egos and Silos Be Gone!

What kills some organizations these days is the inability to get along across departmental silos—or just plain get along. The brandful workforce is a concept that absolutely requires collaboration and a "let the walls come down" approach. Each expert in an organization must value the other perspectives and know that no one expert will reign. They all must move to the beat of the same drum—and be united by a common goal, the purpose of the organization. As well, everyone needs to be on the same page in terms of the organization's culture, beliefs, mission, business strategy and brand, which are all interchangeable. For example, if the new marketing campaign does not resonate with the employees and they are not jazzed about it, this could be a red flag. More teamwork, communication, and integration need to happen to bring everyone into the fold.

Does your organization have both prerequisites, including CEO buy-in and a culture of collaboration? Share your comments here or read others at http://brandfulworkforce.com/book/general-discussion.

The Road Map Unveiled

My quest for answers on how to build a brandful workforce took me to hundreds of discussions with executives, managers, and frontline employees across many disciplines, industries, and settings. I was more determined than ever to get some answers as I found myself on a journey to find the golden nugget—the holy scriptures of brandful workforces. Armed with experience, curiosity, and determination, I arrived at a simple two-step process on how to build a brandful workforce, depicted in the diagram on the following page.

This section and the next section detail each part of the road map, but here's a quick summary. Simply put, no employee is going to promote a product or service that's failing. The first phase in the road map boils down to walking the talk. This is easier said than done. All organizations start out and continue with a plan—a plan about your purpose, and how to be and remain profitable and competitive. It also describes what you're going to deliver and how. The plan may look good on paper. It may even look great. Maybe even stupendous! But then comes...drum roll please...execution. This is where it may get a bit shaky. Are you doing what you said you were going to do? Is it working? Your plan sets expectations in the minds and hearts of your employees and customers, both of whom impact the success or failure of your organization.

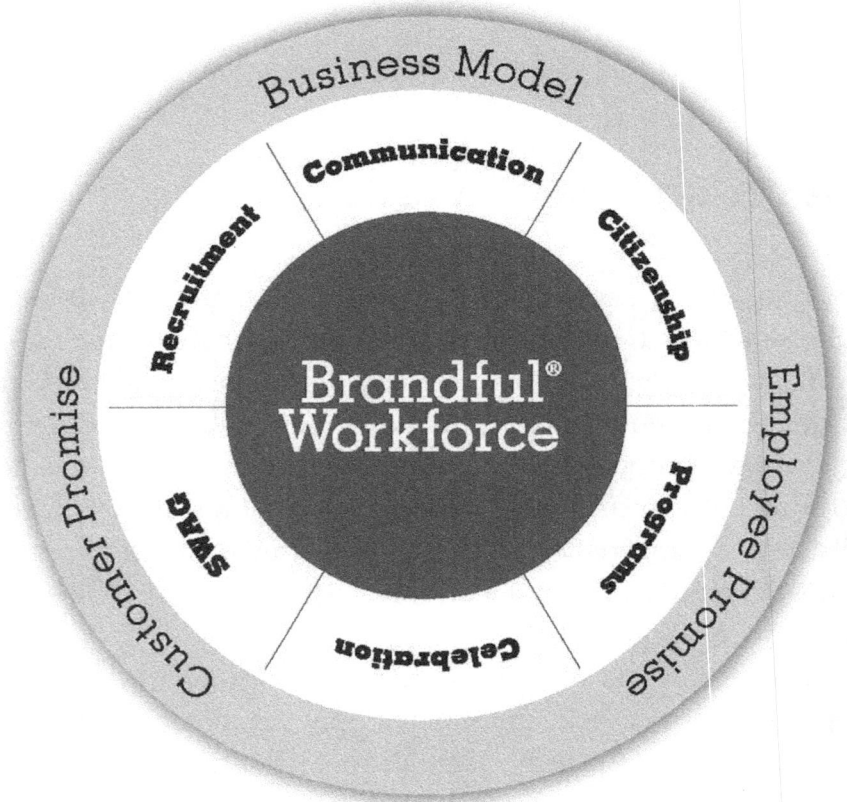

Phase 1 (The Outer Circle): Have a Compelling Business That Works
(Successful business model + customer promise + employee promise)
Phase 2 (The Inner Circle): Provide a Way for Employees to Promote the Brand
(Employees can be brandful through six channels: communication, celebration, programs, recruitment, swag, and citizenship.)

The second phase is one that most folks miss altogether—providing tools, resources, and venues for employees to actually be brandful. The common mistake I see here is that organizations are trying to train employees to be brandful, instead of simply providing easy-to-use resources and outlets that can be used naturally by employees who truly love the products and services they help deliver. The job of folks in marketing, advertising, corporate communications, and citizenship is quite simple—once you have a good profitable business. It's interesting to see that some of these folks don't realize that their success is due, in part, to being in a great organization with a bright future.

The Brandful Workforce Model Ended My Quest for Simplicity

Complexity is a top roadblock to organizational success, whether for big or small organizations. For employees to be cheerleaders in your organization means that you really do have it all right! They know all the internal dirty laundry and they still love the organization. They believe in the product or service. It's not a scam. It's a real need being filled with a smart business model and niche. Marketers shouldn't have to be liars. Nobody should be. To get away from complexity, a brandful workforce offers a commonsense, *very simple* approach to not only a successful business, but a workforce that promotes the business.

Each of these steps and their components will now be reviewed in more detail.

TWO

How to Build a Business Employees Want to Promote

Brandful Business Basics

*N*obody will want to promote an organization whose products or services are going down the tubes.

Your Business Model

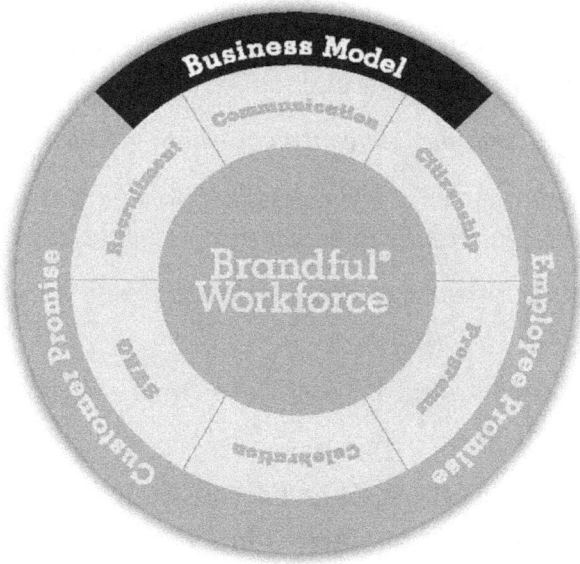

Build Something Employees Want To Promote

I remember the first time I ever walked into a Trader Joe's. I had a feeling, while strolling my cart up and down the aisles, of discovery, exploration, and fun. I was in a grocery store full of new products waiting to be tried. And everything looked enticing. And the prices—wow—less than what I'd normally pay at the typical supermarket. It seemed that everything about Trader Joe's was different. They had figured out the hardest and most important part of any successful organization—the business model.

When you look at Trader Joe's website, they don't necessarily say this is their business model, but it's their answer to *How do we do it?*

- *We buy direct from suppliers whenever possible, we bargain hard to get the best price, and then pass the savings on to you.*

- *If an item doesn't pull its weight in our stores, it goes away to gangway for something else.*

- *We buy in volume and contract early to get the best prices.*

- *Most grocers charge their suppliers fees for putting an item on the shelf. This results in higher prices…so we don't do it.*

- *We keep our costs low—because every penny we save is a penny you save.*

- *It's not complicated. We just focus on what matters—great food + great prices = Value.*

That, in a nutshell, is what I'd call their business model: *a long-term sustainable business plan that is financially, ethically, and socially successful. From the perspective of a brandful workforce, a business model not only consists of how you are successful, but also who you are—your brand.* In looking further at Trader Joe's, you can see a big company, unique personality, a story, and what they stand for: *innovative, hard-to-find, great tasting food.* I'm not an expert on creating and sustaining a successful business model; however, I know this is absolutely essential for a brandful workforce.

So, why would Trader Joe's be so transparent and put their business model on their website for all to see? Aren't they afraid of someone trying to copy them? Maybe they have been copied or are being copied right now. Does it matter? They have already built up a solid reputation and consistent delivery. Every business has to be careful of the competition and potential challenges. What makes for a good business model today might not be a good business model tomorrow. So making it clear to others, especially at a high level, may not pose as big a risk as one might think. Also, having a great business model and being able to execute on it are two different things. They have the experience and knowledge to do that, whereas someone else may not.

A failing business model is usually the reason behind a failing business, but other areas of the business typically get blamed. Business models can easily become outdated, ineffective, or difficult to communicate or execute. And while they are the backbone to any good business, it amazes me how easily others are blamed for a failing business. I've seen fingers pointing at human resources (*you're not bringing in the right people*), or marketing (*you're not selling to the right audience*), operations (*you're not delivering on what we promised*). In fact, it's the business model itself that is crashing. While it is possible for a brandful workforce to save a sinking business—for example, they work for reduced wages, they pitch in where needed beyond their scope—it is not sustainable unless the organization can really figure out how to provide their products or services over the long term. It really should be that simple, and kept that way.

Further defining a business model, it is how your organization is either profitable—or, for nonprofit organizations, able to carry out your cause within a budget. This includes whom you serve (your customer), what you serve, how you make a profit or maintain a budget, and how you are different from or the same as competitors in your industry. As well, it includes a description of the organization's mission, which is the reason for existence, other than just to make money. The business model should be good for more than the short term, and regularly refreshed as any of these important ingredients may be threatened due to the changing competitive landscape or another factor. The business model should also answer the question: *Does the organization plan to grow or stay the same over time?*

Now that we have looked at what defines a business model, for the purposes of building a brandful workforce, let's look at why it's a critical component of Brandful Business Basics. The business model serves three purposes for building a brandful workforce.

1. *It forms the basis (along with customer and employee promises) upon which employees can be brandful. It serves as a focal point for which the customer and employee promises can be built.*

2. *It unites the workforce toward a common purpose (throughout the organization). It answers the question, why are we here? And it engages employees to be brandful—they can act like owners and citizens, and participate more fully and appropriately in the brand.*

3. *It attracts and retains brandful employees.*

Let's look at each one.

Your business model is really the basis of a brandful work-force—the *what* and the *why* they are promoting. Let's face it. When an organization starts out as an idea, it's simply an idea. It becomes a business model when it's financially feasible and sustainable—or at least someone believes it is and will be. That's the part that has to get done first; however, it's not complete without thinking about the customer and the employee. For your business plan to be effective, somebody has to execute the business plan—the employees—and somebody has to purchase or receive the product or service—the customers. Putting these pieces together will help define what kind of employees you need to deliver your products and services to your customers.

Another reason the business model is so critical to a brandful workforce is that it unifies the workforce as a powerful voice of the brand. Each employee is part of a whole, that together is able to offer a product or service that would not be possible from a single individual. No matter how big or how small the organization, whether it's staffed by volunteers or paid employees, the workforce joins together with a common purpose. That sense of unity originates in the business model, and can make for powerful brand promotion. For example, Whole Foods unifies its workforce toward the importance of healthy eating.

A clear and well-communicated business model can help attract and retain brandful employees. Every day is a choice. You want to keep it that way. I see more and more managers complain about complacent employees. Your employees should be there because every single day, they choose you. Having a good business model, and evolving it to remain competitive and up-to-date, gives your employees the motivation to make that choice every day. A good business model also can serve as a magnet for new employees. It most likely won't be the determining factor—but it can help.

Employees do care about your business model.

Employees not only want some stability knowing the organization will be around in the future, they want to be an active part of the evolving business model, and provide their input and ideas. They don't just work there, they are also vested like shareholders—but they can't just sell if it goes down. They want to tell their friends and family about it. It's a source of pride. For example: *My employer is doing great!* versus *My employer just laid off a thousand employees and I may be next.*

Employees also like to know that their jobs are there for a reason—every job is absolutely needed for the business to run effectively and efficiently. If it's not needed, it should be eliminated. Why would any employer hire for a role that was not needed? Sometimes when I talk to friends or colleagues and I mention this, I am amazed that some folks don't realize how much their employers truly need them. I ask: *Why would your organization pay you, if they didn't need you?* There's so much analysis these days to determine what jobs, roles, and skills are needed to provide the products or services. Today, more than ever, every person does make a difference. When every employee really understands the value of his or her contributions toward the mission, toward making the execution of the business plan a reality, it becomes quite powerful—and actually motivates the employees to promote the brand as if it's not just a job, but part of a bigger force.

Now, let's look at a couple of examples of how the business model is critical to building a brandful workforce.

JetBlue

When JetBlue was created, it had a solid business model that was almost guaranteed success. It started with low costs and high efficiency (aircraft utilization) that beat the competition. JetBlue's founder had figured out a way to enter the market with a huge competitive advantage. He knew that other airlines would come in and try to undercut JetBlue's low prices, but he knew that JetBlue would make a profit charging low prices, and the other airlines would have to take a loss in their attempt to stamp out JetBlue. While this strategy is how airlines usually prevent other airlines from successfully starting, JetBlue's strategy was also to focus on the sore spot of airline transportation–customer service. People were thrilled to see a new airline, with low prices and exceedingly better customer service, with a hub in New York City. "Bringing humanity back to air travel" really touched an emotional chord and JetBlue was an immediate success—not only with customers, but employees.

IAM—Interfaith Assistance Ministry

Nonprofit organizations also have successful business models. Some nonprofits, such as IAM in Hendersonville, North Carolina, are able to attract funding and volunteers more easily than others. That's because of the business model. People can volunteer in a slew of organizations, but why is it that they all want to volunteer in one particular place in Hendersonville? Because they can personally feel the difference they make and they love that feeling. At IAM, a nonprofit that provides emergency relief and resources to Henderson County residents in financial crisis, *volunteers offer a hand up and not a hand out.* I spoke with IAM's executive director, who proudly shared that, because of their volunteers, they are able to return $2.04 for every dollar donated, which I understand is higher than most nonprofits. Note that nonprofits measure their financial success, just as the private sector does. Their people, whether they are employees or volunteers, want to know that their efforts are making a difference.

At IAM, volunteers take on responsible and critical roles, not just behind the scenes, but in areas such as reception and interviews with clients, which they say is satisfying and impactful. They have three hundred volunteers and some have been around for over twenty years. The volunteers appreciate what IAM is all about—and possibly more importantly, *how* they do it. They also have confidence in the way IAM puts donations to use, whether it be food, clothing, or cash. Volunteers are said to *distribute what the heart of the community provides.* At IAM, 95 percent of staff are volunteers, and are often believed to be paid staff members because of their professionalism.

One of the brandful volunteers went so far as to write an article in the local newspaper, raving about the organization as one of his favorite nonprofits, saying:

> *It means so much to me to be a volunteer at IAM...I enjoy helping others and problem solving. The [volunteer] job of intake interviewer allows me to do both. Training provided at IAM is excellent, and the staff members treat you as their best friend. All your fellow volunteers have smiles on their faces and generous, warm hearts.*

But what if your organization's business model is in question? There may be hope for some failing business models.

Certain challenging industries, known for failing business models—such as the recently failing higher education business model in the United States—might not be able to attract employees, especially if folks are savvy in choosing an employer based on its business model. But let me be clear: just like folks invest in stocks when they are down because they have faith they'll go up, candidates can be interested in a failing organization or industry if they believe they are on the mend or have an innovative plan for the future. And any industry can have a new entrant that is successful, like JetBlue when it entered the tumbling airline industry. What other industry do you know that charges less than it did twenty years ago? The game continues to evolve. New creative entrepreneurs enter the scene constantly and come up with better, more efficient and creative ways to conduct business using the latest technology.

Let me return to my mention of the failing business models as it pertains to higher education. A recent discussion pointed to universities as having beefed up their marketing campaigns as a way to get more applicants. Don't they understand that marketing campaigns don't stand a chance when the cost of tuition has outpaced inflation and that the educational landscape has changed? They could have the best marketing campaign in the world and still not be able to attract more students. It's not the marketing, it's the business model. Folks are wondering if it's worth it. A college degree may mean a higher paying job; however, you are in debt for the rest of your life. Now, it's easier than ever to learn what you need to on the job or through other channels like mentoring, online classes, certificates, courses, and internships.

Take Jennifer Turliuk, who went on a quest to figure out what she wanted to do in life after she finished college. Instead of attending graduate school, she decided to put herself through what she lists on her LinkedIn profile as a "Self-Education Program." Most students don't have the practical training as part of their college education (or high school) to prepare for and choose a career or job. Jenn knew she wanted to start her own business, so she e-mailed people directly and asked to informally speak to them about their jobs and shadow them. In the process she was able to learn from them, and found some courses she could attend for free. She spent three months, and instead of obtaining a graduate degree, she really honed in on aligning her interests with viable opportunities. Not that there are many folks like Jenn out there, but is this kind of path going to be a viable alternative to graduate education? And will this or something else force the business model of higher education to change? Do the employees of higher educational institutions worry about their future? I wonder if it might be challenging for them to promote their organizations.

Having a good business model is essential, and is step one. But don't stop there. You must communicate it at a high level and encourage your employees to understand it and *get it* so they can become active promoters. Tweet-sized sound bites of your business model need to be easily understood and communicated in daily conversation. Not the details. High level. We don't need to know how Trader Joe's had the lowest cost and all the details, but just the fact that they figured it out and have a solid plan. The employee population generally needs to know the plan. That's not to say that backup and details are not important. They just aren't critical for mass communication.

For example, I had a feeling that the business model was solid at Wegmans, a privately owned supermarket chain, headquartered in Rochester, New York. But I tested out my hypothesis while shopping at one of their New York locations. I asked the check-out clerk if Wegmans had a bright future. His eyes lit up and he started rambling on and on about what a fantastic company it is and that management *knows exactly when and where to open a new store. They have the recipe down pat!* he told me convincingly. He proceeded to tell me that they only open three stores per year, to guarantee they are all successful. As well, he knew more about the financials of the company than I had expected.

This example hits home. If you don't have a clear business model, then how are the employees not only going to be able to promote it, but be jazzed to do so?

Beware: The Kiss of Death

Organizations that teeter on the brink of profitability, due to a slipping business model, often run the risk of abandoning everything that doesn't have to do with making money. And yes, I get it, and I'm the first to admit that without profitability there is no business. But you cannot abandon the mission, the purpose, the raison d'être, that goes beyond profitability. Having a good business model allows the organization to not solely focus on profits or a budget. For when a company is trapped into this *profitability trance*, it can become the kiss of death. Employees will not see any meaning, mission, or sense of purpose, and they will lose the emotional connection. If you have to focus too heavily on being profitable, then it's not a good business model. Get one you are confident in and will allow you to fulfill greater meaning.

This section was not meant to dive any deeper into creating a business model. It's simply pointing out that a business model is critical for building a brandful workforce. Does your organization have products or services that you want to promote? Please share your comments and read others at http://brandfulworkforce. com/book/brandful-business-basics/business-model.

Business Model Checklist

Here's a handy checklist you can use to determine if you are ready to move on:

- ❑ Is my organization profitable, or do we have a plan to be profitable in the near future?

- ❑ Can I summarize how my organization is profitable in one minute?

- ❑ Can other employees do the same? Do they?

- ❑ Does my organization keep employees updated as the business model changes?

- ❑ Is my organization's business model integrated with:

    - ❑ my employee strategy?

    - ❑ my differentiated customer promise that will keep customers loyal?

Now, let's look at the promises—customer and employee.

What's a promise?

A promise is a commitment to follow through on what you said you would deliver. Sure, stuff happens, but a promise is a promise. Fulfilling a promise builds trust. Don't create a promise without intending to fulfill it. Do what you say. Say what you do.

Your Customer Promise

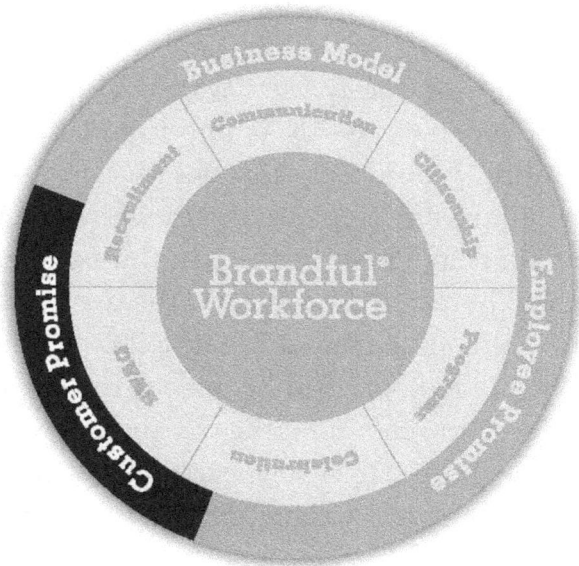

Employees deliver the customer promise every day. They bring your business to life. Every employee either serves a customer or serves another employee who serves a customer. They must know the customer promise and stand behind it, if they are going to deliver it. But they can go even further: employees have the power to go beyond the promise and delight—that's the power of being brandful.

Executives cannot possibly plan or control every possible customer interaction; however, they can provide a framework for the ideal customer experience, sort of a goalpost. Or another way to say this is: Executives have their repertoire of preferable plays, but the employees control the ball or puck. The team agrees on a great play ahead of time, but when they are actually on the field, circumstances may call for a quick change to the plan that allows for an unforeseen goal. If this happens, go for it! It's the same thing at work.

Here's a headline: *Airline Delays Flight for Man to See His Dying Mom.* While the airline industry is one full of regulations and standard operating procedures, and one that measures success based on timely arrivals, employees actually went against their normal routine to help a man in need. In this situation, the man was able to make the last flight of the day (because the airline held the plane for him) and arrived at the hospital in time to say his last good-bye to his mother. Had he missed the flight, he would not have been able to see his mother as she passed away early that next morning. While this is one example of employees going against the business model (reliability, being on time), there are many others. No employee guide or customer service guide could spell out how to handle these situations. When employees have true compassion for others and when the situation is ripe, one person can make a big difference in the lives of others. And it's these stories that help make the brand come alive.

While the example above was not JetBlue Airways, there are plenty of these kinds of stories at JetBlue as well as other airlines and companies. Having worked mostly in back-office roles, I do remember one of my greatest customer service moments when I participated in a Holiday Helper program at JetBlue. Corporate employees went to the airport to help out during the holiday rush of customers. Prior to working at the airport, I had heard the many JetBlue stories of helping customers. JetBlue had done a great job at spreading the customer compliments that had come thanks to the compassion and commitment of the Crewmembers. I was thrilled to be able to experience it firsthand and assist the customers personally. I vividly remember this one family that had arrived late to the airport. They were traveling to San Juan to spend Christmas with their relatives. I saw them arriving with a look of panic on their faces. They had two small children and I went up to them to help. I was able to personally escort them through security and get them to the gate just before the doors closed. Just seeing the look of complete gratitude on their faces, knowing they had made it, gave me a feeling that I'll never forget. Wow—to be part of an organization that allows employees to truly help the customers is quite a feeling.

Here's another example from a single employee that goes above and beyond standard customer expectations. When I walked into Financier Pastry Shop and asked about the level of sweetness in the chai latte, unsure if I'd like it, I was offered one on the house. The server told me to try it and if I liked it, I'd come back for more. Was the server allowed to do that? Was he breaking a rule or was he empowered to make that decision? Was Financier calculating how many freebies they were giving—to be sure it was not hurting profitability? What if it was helping profitability and was part of the business model?

Delivering the customer promise does not necessarily require a set of policies or a guidebook. It's something that comes from deep inside, and that is what being brandful is all about. Instead of a policy, it's more of a matter of principle. At JetBlue, there are five leadership principles, and one is "Doing the Right Thing" as opposed to "doing things right." Since employees are in unique situations daily, they really have to be able to think on their feet and make decisions in line with the company values, principles, and purpose.

Emphasize high level.

In order to get behind it and deliver it, just as employees need to understand the high-level business model, they should also understand the high-level customer promise. I want to emphasize *high level*. There's only so much that any given employee can take in. It's too easy to be overwhelmed with too much information and then lose focus on what's most important. There are plenty of books on customer experience, how to build one that is exceptional, and how to maintain it. We will not go there; rather, we will focus on what's most important to the brandful workforce.

To be brandful and truly promote the products and services of the organization, employees need a customer promise that they can:

- *understand*

- *fulfill*

- *critique and shape*

Let's look at each one of these.

I Need a Customer Promise that I Can Understand

If you don't have a customer promise, there's no goalpost for the employees. Many organizations don't have a customer promise because they either can't agree on one, they don't believe one customer promise can last over time, or they don't want to hold themselves accountable to one. One other possible excuse might be that they simply don't know how to create a customer promise.

Some of the customer promises that do exist are too complicated. Here's a real customer promise I found online:

We promise:
- *To be your advocate*
- *To have the best prices*
- *To offer the largest selection online*
- *To be available*
- *To charge no fees*
- *To remain unbiased*
- *To make it simple*

Each one of these has more detail, but by the time you get to the last one, it's not so simple anymore. There are too many for any one person to focus on.

A customer promise needs to make sense, and be aligned with the business model. Some organizations have a simple and commonly accepted customer promise, such as TD Bank. I believe it can be summed up in one word: convenience. Yes, there is a lot that is packed into this customer promise; however, it all can be simplified into this one bucket. And convenience is their main differentiator and competitive advantage. They are open longer hours. They provide pens when customers have complained of pens being chained to the counter. They allow pets in the bank. Everything they do is associated with providing convenience to customers. Whatever your business model depends on should be addressed in your customer promise.

For other organizations like Coca Cola and Maker's Mark, their customer promise is their product or recipe, the great taste that customers have come to love. When they each changed their recipes for the soda and bourbon respectively, they got a customer backlash—and reverted back to their original recipes. But they were lucky. They had created such a huge fan base of customers who had made their brands a part of their daily lives. Other organizations with lesser established relationships would have had customers leave without comment. Loyal customers know what they are getting and anything different is not acceptable. Delivering on your promise time after time is what builds a good brand. Failing to deliver on your promise is what builds a bad brand.

So what is a customer promise? It's an expectation of what your product or service is and how you deliver it to your customer. It defines your entire customer experience.

The customer promise, if understood correctly, serves as a focal point for all employees, as to what can be achieved. When they truly see it in this way, their attitude becomes quite attentive to the customer needs. I've seen employees with a competitive attitude pitting themselves against the customer. They sometimes complain: *The company does everything for them and nothing for me.* Some employees resent having to serve the customer. However, when they understand that the customer promise is what keeps everyone in business, the customer is typically not seen as a burden, but an honor to delight. A simple and clear customer promise helps every employee connect what they do to the overall success of serving the customer.

I Need a Customer Promise That I Can Fulfill

Now that the goalpost is clear, how do we get the ball through? Is the organization's customer promise something we can bring to life?

Ritz-Carlton's customer promise is to provide the finest personal service and facilities where genuine care and comfort of guests is the highest mission. The company allows its "ladies and gentlemen" (their employees) to spend up to $2,000 on a guest per incident (not year) *We entrust every single Ritz-Carlton staff member,* *without approval from their general manager, to spend up to $2,000 on a guest. And that's not per year. It's per incident...The concept is to do something, to create an absolutely wonderful stay for a guest.* This approach puts the employees in a position to be able to deliver on the company's promise.

Another example is a tool that Lowe's introduced (with help from Apple) for their employees to be able to better serve customer needs directly, without having to involve a manager. The Lowe's employee app gives store staff access to key product information, and includes a bar-code scanner and credit card reader. By putting more information and functionality in the hands of the employees, employees are enabled to deliver the kind of customer experience that their brand promises.

The Spanish retailer Zara's success can be attributed to their supply chain speed and customer-centric approach. Clothes move from concept to design to stores within days. But the real secret seems to be their pulse on the customers, which comes through— no, not a customer survey, but rather, their employees. While most organizations have a centralized customer team that is usually in charge of customer surveys and feedback, among other responsibilities, Zara zeroes in on employees who contact headquarters daily with customer needs. If someone wants a shirt in a certain color, that information gets transmitted immediately. How empowering is that for an employee to be able to advocate on behalf of the customer and provide quick results? The entire process is a win-win for the company and for employees.

An employee at the Apple flagship store on Fifth Avenue in Manhattan once told me that they are empowered to ensure that every customer that walks into an Apple store leaves happy. They have the tools and resources available to directly resolve issues with the customer, without having to call on a supervisor or manager. They are trained to solve customer problems, not sell them products. Their promise of sleek, simple, and easy to use translates from paper into reality via the store design as well as the store employees.

Give employees what they need to deliver your customer promise, and they might just delight them.

I Need a Customer Promise that I Can Critique and Shape

When I really understand the customer promise and can deliver on it, I also see firsthand when something is not working or needs to change.

Why would there be *change*? That's the one thing we can all count on: change. With this in mind, your employees should be seen as helpful to identifying barriers and presenting solutions to the integrity of your customer promise. You should not only want their input, you should depend on it.

Where are employees in your customer experience map? Is your map a circle, a line, a ladder, or something else? Is there a way for employees to provide valuable, practical information on areas that impact the customer experience? For example, they may say, *I know that our promise is X and I was unable to deliver that because of Y. I propose we do Z to resolve it.* Employees are instrumental in informing you about the disconnects in your customer promise. Here's an example of a disconnect that I see quite often: The customer promise is quick service, but they fail to provide enough staff to deliver on that promise. Or maybe customers who used to care mostly about service start caring more about quality, so your promise doesn't match what the customers want. Employees are often placed in a bad position, fail to deliver the promise, or are focused on the wrong promise. Employees can also help you segment your customers. They personally know which customers are your best, most loyal and most engaged.

Help them help you.

When an organization is under pressure to make short-term fixes to remain profitable, focus easily shifts away from the customer, who is actually the reason for profitability, and more toward financial statements. Employees can help you maintain focus on what's important. Changes are necessary; however, engaging in dialogue with employees is critical to maintaining integrity and the ability to execute.

Again, help them help you.

Customer loyalty depends on employees, whether the organization delivers a product or service. Most folks think that a brandful workforce is geared toward customer service industries; however, organizations that produce products also stand to gain. The employees behind the scenes who make the products impact the quality, efficiency, and overall brand—which all factor into customer loyalty.

I am starting to see that experts in customer loyalty, customer experience, customer satisfaction, and customer analysis are turning to the workforce more and more to find answers. They are beginning to see that the root of their success is the employee. Whether they realize it or not, customer experience is dependent on employee behavior and attitude.

The power of being brandful.

Before we end this part, I'd like to tell you about an employee that delivered more than the customer promise. Zamir, a Dunkin' Donuts employee in Stony Brook, New York, established a special bond with his customers, transcending the usual customer relationship. He works the night shift, and over the years has come to know many of the local university students. About sixty students, on their own initiative, made a video (View the video at— http://youtu.be/X90AGu6t1Lo) to thank Zamir for his compassion for them and his service at Dunkin Donuts. When you watch the video, you immediately understand that there is a strong connection between this one employee and his customers—a connection that no guidebook could have influenced.

Do employees at your organization have a special bond with customers? Share comments at http://brandfulworkforce.com/book/brandful-business-basics/customer-promise.

Is your customer promise good enough to support a brandful workforce? Below is a handy checklist to help you to make the determination.

Customer Promise Checklist

- ❑ Do frontline employees know the customer promise?

- ❑ Is my customer promise integrated with the business model?

- ❑ Is my customer promise integrated with the employee promise? (see next section)

- ❑ Are employees easily able to deliver on the customer promise?

- ❑ Do employees communicate out the customer promise?

- ❑ Do employees get upset when they cannot deliver the customer promise?

❑ Do employees speak up when they cannot deliver the customer promise?

❑ Are employees behind the customer promise 100 percent?

❑ Does my customer promise deliver the business results I expect?

❑ Is my customer promise realistic for employees to deliver consistently?

Your Employee Promise

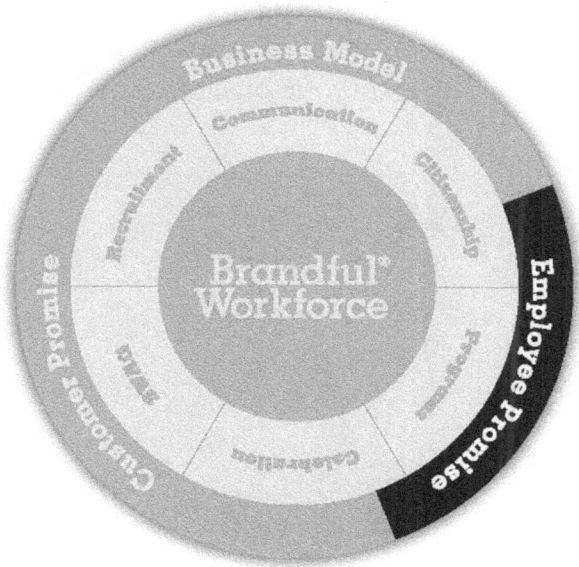

If you think an employee promise is simply salary and benefits, you are mistaken. If that's all you provide, then that's all they will ever care about.

Think for a moment about what your organization offers to employees for their hard work. What typically comes to mind are pay and benefits. Traditionally, this is what the exchange looks like. The employee is given a job to do and is paid in return. Sound simple? It's not. Why? Because people are humans, not robots. There are certain jobs that you wouldn't take no matter how much you were paid. And there are certain jobs you would do for almost nothing.

There's so much more to it.

Where does an employee promise start? With a pyramid, of course. Doesn't every good book have one? An employee promise starts with your mindset, your philosophy about your employees...and how they fit into your business model and customer promise.

My employees are a
critical part
of my organization's brand

My employees do not matter
at all to my organization's brand

What is your people philosophy? How do you value the workforce? What role do they play in the organization's success? I'd like to propose a hierarchy in terms of an organization's people philosophy. At the bottom of the pyramid is simple survival. The philosophy would be along the lines of: *Anyone can work here.*

Everyone is replaceable, so just get me anyone with a pulse who's willing to do the job. Turnover is a given. People are just the luck of the draw. You can never count on anyone anyway.

You need to be careful. Even though an organization's people philosophy may not actually be at the bottom of the pyramid, the approach and method of communication can make it appear that way. Take a look at this real quote from an incoming CEO at a global organization trying to rebuild a broken business:

...anyone unable to support the [organization's new] plans should resign. My message to those people [the employees] is simple, [our company] is not the place for you. The rules have changed. You won't feel comfortable here and, to be frank, we won't feel comfortable with you as colleagues.

Similarly, many employees are currently of this mindset: *I'll just stick it out another couple of weeks at this hell-hole, until I find something else.* Which came first? the employee mindset or the CEO's? Post your thoughts at http://brandfulworkforce.com/book/general-discussion.

At the top of the pyramid, which represents a more evolved thinking, the philosophy would be along these lines: *People are the reason for our success. We know exactly what kind of people bring us success and, in turn, love it here.* This brandful workforce hierarchy should allow you to clearly see whether or not your organization is ready for a brandful workforce. Being at the top of the pyramid doesn't mean that you pay employees through the roof. It simply means that you have an employee promise that matches two needs: the needs of your business and the needs of the employees you hire. And the reason you have an employee promise is that you believe that not all workers are created equal, and you need to be picky about finding the right match for your organization.

Let's look at a few examples of organizations that believe employees are critical to their brand. The Container Store, a retailer that began in 1978 in Texas, demonstrates their philosophy in much of what they do. They have been referred to in the the media as *putting people before profit*. They take care of employees so the employees can take care of the customer. From the beginning of operations, The Container Store has depended on its employees to move the company forward. They attribute much of their success to their employees.

At Urban Express, a New York City–based courier service, they say:

People first…We look at it this way: If we treat our team well, they will stick around and get better at what they do, feel more responsibility for their actions, and strive to grow and improve at their jobs. And that means our business as a whole will grow and improve and so will our service to you, our clients. Instead of instant karma, it's more like a lifelong investment in relationships that pays off in many more ways than one.

How do you reveal your people philosophy? Is it part of your business model and mission? GE Aviation had a commercial that featured employees being taken to the runway to see the takeoff of an aircraft, which had an engine that the employees had designed. It connected their achievement and hard work to the aircraft flight. Their pride was the feature of the television commercial that helped sell GE to its customers. Having employees that care and want perfection is a huge part of the GE brand. This commercial really hits home with the brandful workforce concept. See the video on this YouTube link: http://www.youtube.com/watch?v=ySwp12Rp8Jk&feature=youtu.be.

At JetBlue, the passion demonstrated in an employee-made video shows that the company's people philosophy penetrated through to the front lines, where the employees act and feel like an important part of the brand. The video celebrates the daily progress of employees delivering the JetBlue experience in Long Beach, California. The employees there clearly indicate their solid alignment with the JetBlue core value of Safety, and went so far as to voluntarily make a video about it. And this is a major point of the pyramid. Regardless of what your people philosophy is, it will be seen through the actions and attitudes of frontline employees. See the YouTube video here: http://www.youtube.com/watch?v=fR0el4JwZZI.

What is an employee promise?

Now that we've seen the people pyramid, let's turn to the question: What is an employee promise? First and foremost, it is where your business model and customer promise intersect. This intersection defines the type of employee needed to carry out your mission, fulfill your business model, and deliver on your customer promise. Second, the employee promise differentiates you from other employers. Some organizations start and end with the employment differentiators instead of with the business. But, if you don't connect your employees to your business, you risk not having the right workforce to be able to succeed.

An employee promise is the backbone of an organizational culture. It tells you what's valued, how the work gets done, and by what kind of people. An employee promise enables the organization to find and hire the right folks that will propel the success of the organization. How do organizations operate without one? It astonishes me that very few organizations have a sensible, clear, defined, consistent and relevant employee promise…that is also executed accordingly.

The employee promise is commonly the missing link to building a brandful workforce.

Employees need the employee promise too, as they need to know what they are being provided and what's expected of them. It helps them make a decision on whether to take a job or whether to stay employed. It helps them decide for themselves whether they are a good match. Without an employee promise, there is a disservice done to both the employee and the organization.

What not to do.

Some organizations make it seem that almost anyone can work there. Here is how a large global retailer phrases it: *No matter what your talents and interests, you could find your perfect job. With us, of course!* This is not helpful to steering potential employees in a clear direction that your organization needs to be successful. It's true that typical turnover in retail is high; however, this lack of specification cannot help. Sure, it may be difficult to be more specific when there are thousands of roles, but they can do better than this. This global retailer also has scripted videos that appear to be read by their employees. The entire package of the company—from the view of a prospective employee—appears that they'll take anyone looking for a job.

But there are those that are able to be more specific and buck the typical turnover trend by offering and delivering on a compelling promise to their employees. Take Lion's Choice roast beef restaurants in St. Louis, whose average employee tenure is six years. One year, one of the locations had no turnover at all. The average tenure of an assistant manager is twelve years, and seventeen years for the general manager. How do they do it? Their employees love the fact that they know what they're there for. Lion's Choice is very clear on what they provide to and require from their staff, over the long term. And they specifically look to hire folks who are interested in the long term. They focus on a couple of the hot buttons in the restaurant industry: flexibility and scheduling. No employee is required to work over 47.5 hours per week, and they have swing staff available to cover. This system costs a bit more, but they say it pays off big time with the reduction in turnover and training.

Yes, it's true that every organization selects whom they want to hire; however, they should also be just as selective with whom they don't want to hire. The same goes with individual employees choosing an employer. Help candidates choose you for the right reasons, not the wrong reasons.

IKEA bravely communicates what they want and what they don't want in their employees. Both are essential for creating and sustaining a brandful workforce; however, many organizations do themselves a disservice by limiting their search to only what they want. Under Ikea's top ten reasons to work there, number six is:

Egos parked at the door
We're not big on fancy titles, corner offices, or private jets, and we ask co-workers to leave their egos at the door. Why? Because it means you get to work as a team member, have fun, and get on with the job.

Once again: Build your employee promise so that it attracts and retains the right people that can deliver your customer promise and support your business model and mission.

The Four Components of an Employee Promise
- *The job*
- *The typical pay-benefits package*
- *The culture*
- *The brand*

There are four basic components of an employee promise. Each component ties first to running a successful business, and second to differentiating your workplace from others. Three of the components are quite standard (the job itself, the typical pay-benefits package, and the culture) and I will briefly describe these. However, I'm introducing a fourth component: the brand. All four of these have an *exchange* of what the employer provides the employee and vice versa. Even though I discuss this as an exchange, it should not be seen as "tit for tat" or entitlement. It should be seen as honesty, transparency, and authenticity for both employee and employer, not a contract.

First, let's look at the job. The brandful workforce road map does not overlook that first and foremost a workforce exists because a job needs to get done. Therefore, the first part of the employee promise describes the details of a job that's expected of the employee. Every job requires a set of skills, knowledge, and experience (whether it's as minimal as sixteen years of life or as much as an advanced degree with years of experience and specific expertise) needed to get the job done. The exchange part here is that the organization must provide the tools and resources for the employees to get the job done. If I had a dollar for every time an employee was put in a position without the tools or resources to get the job done, I'd be rich.

I caution organizations in creating their job requirements; some are setting the bar too high, unnecessarily, requiring skills and degrees that may not be relevant to getting the job done. When I was hired at JetBlue, nobody cared about my master's degree or my college degree. The founder of the company didn't even have a college degree. (See this list of top entrepreneurs who don't have a college degree: http://www.youngentrepreneur.com/blog/100-top-entrepreneurs-who-succeeded-without-a-college-degree/.) At the time, JetBlue was the "unairline." They specifically were hiring folks without airline experience, as they wanted to be different. Ironically it was harder to get a job offer at JetBlue in 2003—when I joined—than to get accepted to Harvard.

Second, the most widely known component of the employee promise is the typical pay-benefits package. Some call it the *employee value proposition* (EVP), and some view this as the employee promise in its entirety. This includes what the company provides *concretely* to the employee, and the parameters for which the employee can operate. I capture more than just health care, retirement and investing, dental, wellness, tuition reimbursement, etc. and include other areas that are usually taken into consideration and reviewed with an employment decision. These include: commute, hours, vacation, work-life balance, flexibility in schedule, and growth or advancement opportunities. Here is where the employer can start to differentiate themselves from other employers and integrate talent needs with the business model, mission, and customer promise, as in the example above at Lion's Choice.

The third component of the employee promise answers the question: *What kind of individual can thrive in your culture to produce the best results, and what kind of culture are you offering to employees?* It's the work environment. You have a culture, regardless of whether you implemented it on purpose. There is much written and researched on this topic, such as how to build an organizational culture, how to change it, and how to align it with the business. The key in terms of a brandful workforce is ensuring that the culture you say you have really exists, and that you update it as it evolves. It is part of your employee promise, and many employees do sign up to work in organizations specifically because of the culture. A strong culture can be the reason for lower pay (a compromise many make); however, if the expected culture is not there, pay becomes more of an issue.

Cultures differ based on their organizational values, work rules (rigid vs. open; union or non-union), citizenship, involvement (compliant, creative, entrepreneurial), fellow employees, mission, and—most importantly—leadership. The leaders are the ones who model the culture and carry it forward. A colleague of mine once defined culture as "how things get done." As leaders change, so do priorities and the way they get addressed—which is the culture.

Below is an example of how the employee promise intersects with the culture and business model.

A midsize customer service–based organization was struggling to cut costs and make a profit. The CEO thought about reducing his reservation agent staffing and automating the reservation system. But then he realized that the success of his business was due, in large part, to the strong relationships his employees built directly with the customers. Instead of automation, the CEO decided to spend more on reservation agent salaries and focus on these vital relationships, as a key differentiator among his competitors. The decision more than paid off. Cutting the salaries of staffers would have gone against their "relationship" culture, their established employee promise, and their customer promise of being available. In the end, they were trying to establish a better future for their business. Sometimes cost-cutting, especially on people, can backfire. It's best to make business decisions around your people, while focusing on your key business differentiators.

Now, I'd like to introduce the fourth component of an employee promise: the brand. In this case, the brand is the set of products or services the organization delivers, as well as what consumers think about these products or services (and the overall organization). When you think about what kind of talent your business needs to charge forward, why not include the need for people who are truly behind your products and services? Being clear that you want employees who want your brand, specifically, helps connect them to your mission, business model, and customer promise, in a way that the other three components don't. If you don't address your brand—not your employer brand, but your organizational brand—in your employee promise, you risk not being able to create or sustain a brandful workforce. The workforce can be engaged in the job and the culture, but will they be brand advocates? In exchange for their brand promotion (which also means involvement and critiquing and shaping the brand, which every organization can benefit from), employees are afforded brand perks.

Offer an employee promise that includes an exchange whereby employees receive brand perks, and in exchange they get involved in the brand—because they truly are evangelists of your products and services. Such brand perks are both tangible and intangible. Tangible brand perks can be free products or services, or discounted swag (described later), or special events and promotions. Intangible brand perks are associated with the status of a cool brand, whether it be globally, nationally, locally known, or even unknown. If your employees think it's a cool brand, then there are intangible brand perks. When I worked at JetBlue, I was highly regarded among my friends: *Oh, you work at JetBlue!* (eyes wide open, mouth drooling). JetBlue had employees fly inaugural flights, appear at ribbon-cuttings, go to air shows, hear bands at the terminal, and attend special events.

The brand doesn't necessarily need to be cool. It can simply be a brand that the employees appreciate and can get behind. Take Memorial Sloan-Kettering Cancer Center. Their employees are highly dedicated to the cancer work that the organization supports and delivers. Part of their employee promise is that they require all employees to be comfortable in the hospital setting. No matter what the job is—for example, accountant—anyone can be asked to be in the hospital on occasion. At the same time, employees who have loved ones with cancer can be given special employee perks. There is an exchange going on with the brand, specifically.

Organizations that have a clear employee promise that includes the brand get better brand matches than those that don't. A better brand match allows employees to genuinely be brandful.

What differentiates your organization from another, as a place to work?

Now that we've seen how the employee promise connects to the customer promise and supports the success of the business, let's compare, at a high level, how the employee promise can differentiate your organization from others. Some employee promise differentiators can be specific employee interests (like those that relate to your products or services), levels of experience (just beginning, midcareer, or varied career), need for innovators, need for self-starters, flexibility to move geographically, flexibility in schedule or number of hours, or certain personality types. Your employee promise should determine the type of employees you need to get the job done and build a brandful workforce.

First let's look at Whole Foods, a supermarket chain. As an employee, I would be drawn to this organization if I loved fresh food and wanted to work in a company where I could get involved and move up in my career. Their core employee promise focuses on employee involvement and career advancement. Their website showcases how employees are empowered to make decisions. Employees have opportunities to participate by voting. They also have a Team Member Emergency fund to support each other in time of need. Unlike most organizations, they are transparent with career opportunities and even list career paths on their website, so that prospective candidates can explore their career possibilities. Many organizations don't even have defined career paths, but Whole Foods goes as far as to publish them publicly. An employee video boasts: *My job is to replace myself.* Are they serious about career paths or what? Whole Foods connects their employee promise of being involved to advancing its business. In fact, I wonder if their business depends on employee advancement and involvement.

Enterprise Rent-A-Car may be somewhat similar to Whole Foods in that their employee promise centers on career advancement; however, they specifically seek out folks who are just starting out. Enterprise differentiates its employee promise and has been recognized as a great place to launch a career. They offer management training and a wide variety of opportunities. It's a different industry, service-based instead of product-based, and calls for a different set of talent and interest than Whole Foods. It would make sense that a different kind of employee would be able to thrust their business forward versus the kind of employee that would propel Whole Foods. Would you agree? Please share comments at http://brandfulworkforce.com/book/brandful-business-basics/employee-promise.

What about the health care company, Cigna? They look for midcareer folks who want a change and are passionate about making a difference in health. *Experienced professionals* is called out on their career site. *Some of the most successful people at Cigna weren't looking for a career or job change. They were looking to make a difference.*

Your employee promise should be clear in the eyes of your employees so they join and stay for the right reasons. When they join for career opportunities and don't find any, the brand promise is broken. Now, if they change their mind and later don't want the career opportunity but need more flexible schedules, then that's a different story. An employee promise provides your employees with a clear and simple picture of why they should join and why they shouldn't join. You should be able to compare and contrast your reasons with the reasons of another organization. Unfortunately, most organizations do not make it clear; therefore, employees are not really sure what they're getting, outside of pay and benefits.

When I moved from Morgan Stanley to JetBlue in 2003, I knew my needs had changed and I understood I was moving from one employee promise to a completely different one, as the two companies are quite different. In the end, both were great matches for me at different times in my life. At Morgan Stanley, I had made a career transition, and was looking for an organization with a global presence and excellent reputation where I could get training and have potential for advancement. After five years, I realized I wanted to return to more entrepreneurial roots, where I had started prior to Morgan Stanley. JetBlue provided a combination of the entrepreneurial flavor of a start-up and the stability of solid financials. When I joined, it was incredibly innovative, fun, and fresh, and there was plenty of opportunity. I particularly loved the "unairline" rebel approach, and of course I also loved the mission: Bringing humanity back to air travel.

In each case, I had a sense of why I was joining, what was expected, and what was being offered. One was not better than the other. They were simply different and appealed to different interests. The concept is to be clear on who you are and what you're offering.

Anyone for shoes?

Even though I moved from one industry (financial) to another (transportation), organizations in the same industry have tremendous employee promise differentiators. The size of your organization and its maturity level also determine important aspects of your employee promise. Let's look at a few different shoe companies: Nike, Foot Locker, TOMS, Zappos, Footzyfolds, and Blue Elephant.

A global organization like Nike (which has more than shoes, but is being used for illustrative purposes) may appeal to folks who have a true passion for a known or established brand that they truly believe in. Nike may have career opportunities in many locations, and has world-class talent and partnerships. Part of the employee promise is the exposure to the many facets of a large organization, and becoming part of the global brand with billions of dollars in annual revenues. The employee can also be part of a larger Nike mission: *to bring inspiration and innovation to every athlete* in the world. (*if you have a body, you are an athlete).*

Not everyone is drawn to a large, international organization. At the opposite end of the spectrum are smaller mom-and-pop companies like Blue Elephant, in my neighborhood. Interestingly, some current executives got their start at these types of establishments. Part of an employee promise at organizations like Blue Elephant includes hands-on, practical skills that can be applied throughout your career. As well, a workplace that provides employees involvement in all aspects of the business like a jack-of-all-trades can be a big draw for the right kind of person. It's funny to think that Nike could be competing with a small family-owned shop for employees; however, it potentially could happen.

Then there are organizations in between like Foot Locker, an international shoe store chain and TOMS, which is not as interested in profits as they are in providing shoes to needy children around the world. And then there are online shoe sellers like Zappos who focus on customer service. And let's not forget that there are always start-ups on the horizon like Footzyfolds, created by two women who wanted to carry around roll-up shoes in their purses, in the event their heels were hurting their feet. Each organization sells shoes; however, each does it in a unique way, with unique clientele, which all calls for a unique employee promise. Each organization has their pros and cons for potential candidates. And each requires something different from their employees.

At this point, consider whether you are, as an organization, targeting the right employees who are interested in your brand and your differentiated employee promise.

Now, let's turn to a few questions regarding the employee promise that typically arise.

Can an organization be too big or too small to have an employee promise? No. I have heard colleagues at large organizations say: *We're too big to have one employee promise.* I don't buy that. You can still have one; it may just be broader or more general than that of a smaller organization. But there are always general themes about your organization that can be brought together in an employee promise.

Is it all right for my organization to change our employee promise? Yes. Just do it aboveboard, in a way that employees can easily understand and relate to.

I've seen job offers go out and candidates start from day one with a different job than they were offered. This can and does happen. Should there be a renewed promise? If a company is fast-paced and changes quickly, this should be openly discussed as part of the culture and expectations. I've seen some organizations look for employees who like change, or at least are OK with change. They are open and up front with employees, telling them to expect constant change. Candidates who are averse to change are discouraged from joining, as it's part of the promise.

Here are a few questions that you can answer yourself:

When times get tough, can you live up to your employee promise? Do you lay off or do you have other strategies? Do you elicit the help of your employees to find solutions? For example, JetBlue held an internal campaign ("Return to Profitability")—it was the employees who came up with many great ideas on how to save money, as they wanted the company to succeed. Can you ask for voluntary departures or reduced work schedules? How creative can you get? Can you delay hiring, create job sharing, or eliminate certain benefits? The point here is to design your employee promise to withstand tumultuous times.

Does your back office help or hinder your employee promise? Having spent thirteen consecutive years in corporate America, following a few years of nonprofit work, I couldn't complete this chapter on employee promises without mentioning the support of back-office administration. They are the folks that support the managers and supervisors and frontline employees who need to focus on getting the job done. The back-office administration is the behind-the-scenes backbone to delivering your employee promise.

For example, how many times have you been on the telephone with a representative who says: *Oh, I'm so sorry; my computer is very slow today.* Or from another point of view: Health care professionals may be quite passionate about helping their patients get better; however, the administrative details of billing and notes get in the way of doing what they love every day.

There's a real opportunity for the back office to support the employee promise, not put a damper on it. Here's another example: Teachers who love to help children grow often get discouraged—not by the actual work, but by what comes with it: the parents, the school administration, the policies, and the unions. Organizations that do not allow the administration to get in the way of their mission and passion have a better chance of successful branding. A brandful workforce depends on the organization to work in a way administratively that allows the culture, mission, and strategy to be executed flawlessly. When the daily administration is not working (This is where IT, legal, human resources, finance, supply chain, training—all of the support or back-office functions—are critical.), it prevents the execution of the brand from the inside. There's always grunt work. Even artists have to clean up after they complete a masterpiece, but the passion should not be overtaken by the grunt work.

Are you in the right geographical location for your employee promise? You've heard that to build a successful business, what you need is a good location. Well, the same goes for an effective employee promise. Many organizations, rightfully so, internally debate where they should start up, move, or expand. Location is everything—not just for your customer base, but for attracting and retaining the right talent to propel your organization forward. Zappos, the online shoe and apparel company, moved from California to Las Vegas as they needed the right space to offer their services, and grow their brand and talent. I spoke with a recruiting executive from a major financial institution with about 25,000 employees regarding their brand. He mentioned the following:

Our brand is widely known and loved in certain states. As we branch out and open new locations where we are lesser known, the employees in those areas have a different experience with customers. Typically they rave about us; however, in our newer locations, the customers are not as familiar with our products and services, so employees don't get as much instant brand recognition from customers and friends. We can't attract employees as easily in those areas.

Another colleague at a national retail chain confides:

Our headquarters is in a location completely isolated from our stores. There is a cultural disconnect between our store employees and the mothership. We need to relocate to an area where our employees can better mirror our customers.

The last question that typically arises is: *How do I know if my employee promise is working?* Here is a quick test. Which of these two options best reflects the current attitude of your employees?

Option 1: Entitlement

What have you done for me lately?

Option 2: Gratitude

I'm lucky to work here and be a part of this exciting brand.

If you chose the first option, entitlement, it would indicate that you have more work to do on your employee promise. Even though I described a promise as an *exchange*, it is worth noting that nobody should be keeping score. It's more of an understanding based on trust and constant communication. On the other hand, if you chose the second option, gratitude, you're right on. Does your organization have an employee promise? Share more about your response at http://brandfulworkforce.com/book/brandful-business-basics/employee-promise.

For a quick reference, please use the checklist below to evaluate whether your employee promise will support a brandful workforce.

Employee Promise Checklist

Do you have an employee promise that:

❑ you can deliver?

❑ is easy to communicate?

❑ is integrated with your customer promise?

❑ is integrated with your business model?

❑ is currently being delivered upon, according to current employees?

❑ is currently being delivered upon, according to new hires?

❑ is accurately reflected on your website?

❑ includes all four components (details on the specific job, typical pay-benefits package, culture, and brand)?

❑ is being used successfully for recruiting?

Does my employee promise give me a workforce that:

❑ can deliver the customer promise?

❑ can produce business success?

❑ can work in the long term?

THREE

How to Involve Employees in Your Brand

T *ools, like social media, don't make an employee brandful. They facilitate their innate desire to promote the products and services they truly love.*

Warning: Whatever you do—*do not* proceed until you have a great business or have a plan for a great business. If you do proceed anyway, you will be creating brand bashers instead of brandful employees. I have been approached by organizations who want to create a brandful workforce, but want to skip the entire first half of this book. If you don't set your foundation correctly, please don't encourage and empower your workforce to promote your brand. They will take the tools and resources and use it harmfully…do you blame them?

Recently, I conducted an hour-long webinar with 250 organizations. In the middle, at the point where we are right now, I asked them to answer yes or no, whether or not they had the business basics (business model, customer and employee promises) to create a brandful workforce. Fewer than a quarter answered *yes.* How would you answer right now? Vote yes or no at the following link: http://brandfulworkforce.com/book/yop-poll-archive.

Help your employees to share the passion.

On the other hand, just because you have a great business model integrated with your customer and employee promises doesn't mean that your workforce will automatically be brandful and promote your brand. That was just getting the basics in order so that your workforce *can* be brandful. But actually being brandful is another step altogether. The key is to evolve your brand with the help and guidance of your workforce as active participants, as opposed to outsiders. But you can't just call them participants like lip service, they need to be treated as such continuously through their life cycle—from the time they are customers, applicants, candidates, new hires, tenured employees, and alums. Only once they are treated as valuable participants will they behave as such. As a critical part of the brand, they will participate and shape the brand from the inside. ***A brandful workforce is what can sustain an organization through its evolution.***

Don't underestimate the power of your workforce. ***Individual empowerment is on the rise. Not just consumers but employees are gaining control of the brand, too.***

Look no further than right under your nose for help in creating long-term organizational success. Why do most organizations ignore their very own people? Or even worse, they dismiss their ideas, as shown in this comment made behind closed doors by a group of executives: *A frontline employee wouldn't have the proper business training to be able to contribute meaningfully to our business.*

These days, you never know who might be most helpful in promoting your brand and what audience will be most successful. The path of the least investment and the biggest potential bang for your buck is your workforce, which can include volunteers, interns, or students. Surround yourself by those who really believe in what you're doing and they will help spread it. But they need the support. The power of the workforce cannot continue to be overlooked. Just ask the founder of Orabrush, who failed miserably at selling his product in an infomercial, but with the help of a university student became a success after a YouTube video. The video went viral and is what propelled them. Do you have any such employees who can do this for your organization? Sometimes organizations hire folks to do this, but they may not be as passionate, real, and creative as your current employees. If your employees are not like this, maybe you should start thinking about how to either inspire them or hire these kinds of folks.

Employee involvement is more than just participating—it's shaping.

Oh no! Not another employee program. If that's what you think this is, forget about it. It's not.

For employees to be brandful, they need to be involved, which is why this section is entirely dedicated to employee involvement. It's vital to mention—as I did in the opening—that involvement is not just participating in programs that were planned in an ivory tower. It's about being involved in the creation as well. For example, Sony held an employee idea exposition which gave employees the opportunity to present their ideas to the product and marketing teams. A Portuguese bank, Millennium, created a program that invited employees to submit ideas, supported by peers who liked the idea. If it had enough support, it would be reviewed by management for implementation. One more example: LinkedIn started an employee involvement program called "hackdays" that allowed employees to work on creative projects one Friday per month. They have since expanded it for projects that were found to have potential, to allow for employees to work on the project for up to three months. These are just a few examples of real employee involvement in the brand.

A Word About Informal vs. Formal Employee Involvement

Jon Katzenbach of Booz & Company has done some interesting work on the topic of employee involvement. His experience advises that organizations have a combination of informal, grassroots opportunities as well as formal ways—such as established programs run from a main office—for employees to get involved. If organizations have only one kind of involvement and not both, they risk not having a proper balance; they need venues that allow for different kinds of employees to be involved in various ways. The informal venue has few rules, if any. Employees can create projects as they see fit with the approval of a local manager. They are empowered to use local resources and to plan events, exchange ideas, and address key concerns. It's somewhat entrepreneurial. The formal involvement would include specific organized venues like corporate social responsibility outings, employee committees, employee contests, and employee events and programs. Again, both are important; however, they are different. What Katzenbach found is that those organizations that lack the informal may not be as genuine as those that have both.

The Six Brandful Channels For Employee Involvement in Your Brand

When I developed The Brandful Workforce Road Map, I listed out, on several pieces of paper, every single possible way that an employee could promote the brand. The items fell into six channels. This section reviews each one of these in more detail. As you read through, please share your comments and stories from your organization and join in the growing conversation. The six channels are:

- *communication*
- *citizenship*
- *employee programs*
- *celebration*
- *swag*
- *recruitment*

If employees are going to be brandful—actively promote your brand—they can do so through any of the six channels. The most direct and obvious way for employees to promote your brand is through their voices (spoken, written, or otherwise expressed)—but where, when, why, and how the message comes out can vary. From the organization's point of view, the ultimate goal is for employees to *brag* about the products, services, and purpose. All you need to do is provide the outlets for the bragging and draw others into your contagious brand. This happens when employees feel that *my organization is a part of who I am*. Conversely, this also happens when employees are personally offended when someone bashes the organization. They are brandful when they take both success and failure personally and they will defend the organization to infinity and beyond.

Never ever mandate or tell employees to promote the brand. It only happens through:

- *genuine emotional connection.*

- *tools, resources, and support that are easily accessible and available. It's like leaving fruit and nuts on your table instead of cookies and chips for the family to eat. You're not forcing them to eat it, but you're making it available.*

- *well-matched employees who believe in the purpose of the organization and the products and/or services delivered.*

Now let's look at each one of the Brandful Channels.

Channel #1 for Employees to BE Brandful—COMMUNICATION

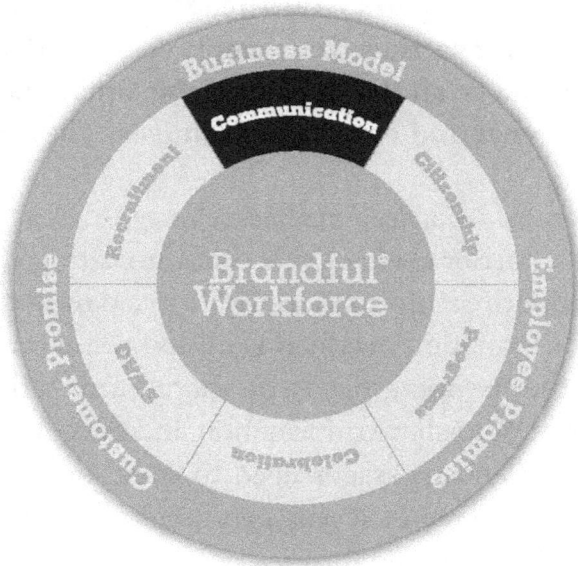

If employees are going to become brand ambassadors, they need to have the proper information and communication channels to get and give the brand messages. *Who's in control of the information flow in your organization?* Or, an even more timely question: *Do you still have control of the communication?* Some argue that organizations need to come to terms with the rise of social media, and the resulting lack of control associated with it. The sooner organizations realize that brands are organic and participatory, the better they will be able to adapt to the changing environment and leverage this toward their success. Those who fight this notion may not be able to keep up. Just as consumers are engaging more and more with the brand and helping to shape it, so too are employees.

Reminder: At this point, you already have a strong foundation from the prior section. Your employees are already jazzed about the products and/or services, the organizational mission, and customer and employee promises. They are ready to promote.

Give Employees a Simple, Repeatable Message.

The biggest barrier to effectively communicating your brand is the overabundance of information. Try to avoid unnecessary communication. Information overload is all too common. Everybody thinks what they're doing has to be shared across the organization. While it's OK to share information and have it available, the important key brand messages need to stand on their own and not be muddled in the mix. It only gets employees frustrated, confused, and unable to spread the message. Keep the brand message simple, focused, and in sync.

Focus communication on key questions every employee should be able to repeat. Questions should pertain to the business model, customer promise, and employee promise such as: *What makes my organization successful and how I am I part of that success? What makes it different from other organizations? What's the mission of my organization? What makes our people unique?* Repeatability is key. Organizations need to constantly communicate the brand internally and externally. Employees need to be reminded of key messages regularly. If it's important, it should be repeated.

The lingo is key to your brand and the repeatability of your message. Does your organization have a certain vocabulary or style of communicating? This should be replicated by your employees, but in their own voices. When I stayed at a themed hotel, every employee ended the conversation with "Take it easy." Rather than sounding natural, it seemed scripted as if they were mandated to use it. What kinds of lingo are being created from the ground up that stick? Employees are now called team members, associates, experts, and specialists. Some organizations have even customized further; for example, employees at Wegmans call themselves *Wegmaniacs,* or employees at IBM are known as *IBMers.* What you do and how you refer to it helps shape your brand—but it has to be genuine.

Communicate Mistakes.

If brands become more sociable and 'human,' they might be able to foster a better and more open relationship with customers.

Encourage everyone to be humble, as it will contribute to your authenticity. Mistakes are human and make your brand real. To understand what I mean, take a look at this excerpt from Scott Friedman's book, *Celebrate!* as told by Rhonda Faught:

> *Bill Richardson was elected governor of the state of New Mexico in November 2002 and took office in January 2003. He appointed me to head the Highway Department. Governor Richardson made it clear that he wanted the Department to be about more than highways. He wanted us to have a commuter rail, statewide transit facilities,*

and be more bicycle friendly…he wanted a multimodal Department of Transportation.

One of the first pieces of legislation passed in Governor Richardson's administration changed our name from the New Mexico State Highway and Transportation Department to the New Mexico Department of Transportation. The law took effect on July 1, 2003.

In preparation for this major change, we had a multimodal transportation summit in Albuquerque, where we invited DOT employees and stakeholders from across the state. It was then that I decided to charge a dollar to each person who said "Highway Department."

At the end of the two-and-a-half day conference, Governor Richardson addressed the attendees with the press present from all the TV stations and area newspapers. He began with, "It's so good to see so many people from the Highway Department here today. Well, I just named the new Highway Commission today…" I couldn't stand it, so I took the microphone away from the governor and said, "Governor…We are NOT the 'Highway Department' anymore. We are a multimodal 'Department of Transportation'—and for that I have to charge you a dollar." The 200+ people in attendance were looking at me thinking: this lady is either really stupid or very courageous. The governor reached into his wallet and pulled out a dollar bill. Then he started talking, and darn if he didn't say "Highway Department" again! Once again, he *pulled out his wallet and handed me a dollar bill. The crowd cheered. Then, for the third time, the governor said "Highway Department." This time he turned to me and said, "I don't have another dollar bill." Everyone in the room went crazy and people were pulling out their wallets, waving dollar bills in the air and saying, "I have one!" I collected $166 that day.*

The headlines the next day said, "Transportation Secretary Fines Governor a Dollar for Saying 'Highway Department.'" I had the article framed with three dollar bills and gave it to him as a gift a few days later.

This was just the beginning. Everyone now knew that we were a multimodal Department of Transportation— we didn't just build highways, but we built and operated transportation systems. Most importantly, the 3000 employees saw our new mission clearly. Soon, I had employees, consultants, and even the general public coming to my office with envelopes of dollar bills, saying they were collecting them from people saying "Highway Department."

Give Employees Access to Information If They Want More Details.
Set your business up so that employees have even more resources than the external press to access information. Employees are stewards of your brand. They depend on clear and concise communication that is more than one direction. If they have a question, there needs to be opportunity for dialogue. Corporate communication departments usually handle all the press calls, but who handles employee calls? In order for employees to truly

be stewards, they need to rely on resources and information in case they have questions about new products, services, announcements, plans, etc. so they can propel the brand forward.

Remember: If done well, communication can position employees to evolve and promote the brand so that it's fresh and real.

Use Multiple Methods of Communication With and Among Employees—Including But Not Solely Focused on Social Media

The communication vehicles are changing quickly, so it's key to be up on which methods of communication your employees utilize the most. And it should be aligned with the communication between employees and customers. If your organization conducts most of your business online, then that's different from a customer service (in-person) business. Or if you have a work-from-home staff or absentee workforce, it's a different angle. Whatever the case, don't waste time communicating in a method that is not utilized. Conway Trucking published a book that was entirely employee voices—it became a keepsake for ongoing inspiration.

Employees can and should be privy to all types of communication, whether it's listening and providing feedback or being involved in the shaping of communication. The reason for this is simple: *It keeps the evolving brand real.* There's nothing worse than an organizational message that falls flat, whether it's local or across several locations. Some types of employee communication are: employee briefings, updates on the business, industry news, the lingo, internal and external campaigns, organizational events, or being privy to customer compliments and complaints.

Support employees who want to learn evolving methods of communication.

Employees are front lines— any one person can be the face. It's about getting them set up and giving them the tools and training to provide a positive foundation. We hire because they are good for the job, but also because they are *influential*. They have networks in their fields—their social circles can make the right kind of impact. For example, the Comcast Cares Twitter account was run by one employee—Bill Gerth. According to *Time* Magazine in 2011, Bill served as "Twitter's most dogged customer-service person."

Educate employees, during orientation or on-the-job, about the evolving communication vehicles so they can learn how the organization shares information and how they can most effectively contribute. IBM was among the first to have employee blogs. Having a communication outlet between and among employees is a great way to spread the message. Thanks to their employees, they often don't need to officially respond to false information in social media as it self-corrects.

Be truly sociable, not just active in social—genuinely interested

A global travel company asked their followers and fans to tell them about their favorite travels. They received a few hundred comments; however, they failed to engage with any of the respondents. They realized it wasn't as easy as simply throwing out some conversation, but they had to keep it going meaningfully. Without making that genuine connection and relationship, it can backfire. This goes for consumers and employees. Some brands can connect more emotionally, like Ford Motor Company. Ford's blog gathers personal customer stories that are inspirational to both customers and employees. One of these is a story of a Ford Mustang owner who bought his car in 1971 and now has over 600,000 miles; he expects it to make it over 1,000,000 miles. He wrote in to the blog advocating Ford as the best motor company and he wanted to share his story.

Here's a synopsis of some conversation that speaks to the human dimension of good brands:

We should encourage brands to consider what they are amplifying through social media. Acting more human begins with connecting through our humanity. That requires honesty and deeper communication. What makes us connect as humans is often vulnerability. Organizations have an identity, fueled by real people who care. They also have honest-to-goodness fears and apprehensions. Those are all human stories worth connecting over. Share something authentic, then ask for something authentic and really listen to the response. There is so much commonality in the world when we take the time to share what matters.

And your employees can help you connect and be sociable, not just active in social media.

Don't Have It all Run by the Marketing or Corporate Communications Team

Brands who do social well don't have it all run by the marketing team. The customer service department is often at the heart of it and can directly relay some stories. Even marketers agree that they are great at many things, but ongoing two-way helpful communications with customers is not one of them. For example, the online travel company mentioned above had its social campaign run by the marketing department. That's not saying to take marketing out of it. Yes, marketing can shape the messages, but there needs to be an integrated loop (that's often missing) to hear the ongoing conversations taking place—to which those in marketing may not always be privy.

Don't incent employees to promote your brand. It should come from them naturally.

Do your employees know the different venues for their communication? What to communicate? How it makes an impact on your organization? This part should be informal. If you provide the information and the resources, it should be natural, not mandated, for your workforce to promote your brand as the opportunities arise. *This should not be over-planned or calculated, or it won't be spontaneous and real.* **If you need an incentive to get employees to be brandful, then something is wrong.** They should be doing it because they really love the product or service. If they don't, then go back and figure out what they don't like and fix that.

Here's an edited excerpt from an organization's experience with communicating the brand internally:

The company launched its first internal blog, with an initial purpose to discuss our brand—"easier"—and build a sense of community among employees. It transformed into much more. How did we do it?

We worked closely with our business partners in legal, human resources, and compliance to get approval to even have an internal blog. We developed a clear governance process outlining how to blog, and terms and conditions for employee engagement and comment approvals. For example, we don't allow anonymous postings, and the weekly blog is monitored by internal communications.

Who would write the blog? Our internal communications folks didn't want an executive or communications person writing it. Instead, our initial blogger was an employee from finance who was interested in the communications field and eager to volunteer. After the first year, we would sponsor a contest and allow employees to vote for their favorite blogger based on sample blog posts.

Let's fast forward. We launched the blog. Participation has steadily increased. Reading is interacting, and we appreciate the lurkers as well as the commenters. Comments on the blog have also increased. We've also seen a huge increase in our blog poll responses.

While many companies have launched internal blogs that didn't work out, here's why ours worked:

- *The author matters a lot. We haven't used an executive or official communications person as the primary blogger. On occasion we have executives participate as guest bloggers, which tends to increase the credibility of the blog and the executive.*

- *Writing style matters. Because the blogger isn't a communications person or an executive, it doesn't read like it was written by one. We use intriguing titles to pull readers in.*

- *Be willing to take on sacred cows. The blog truly is the employee medium and not a corporate mouthpiece. The idea of an internal blog can be scary. We found that our peers at other companies did some lobbying with their business partners just as we did to make it happen. Guess what? Our worst fears didn't come true. Employees know how to behave, and realize what's appropriate in the workplace.*

- *Balance business and fun. Lighter topics help engage employees who are less willing to go out on a limb with an opinion on a business issue. It also helps garner more eyes for topics you really want them to read and talk about later.*

- *Be patient and consider professional help. Sometimes a post may be a dud. Sometimes readership is low. That's OK. Just keep at it.*

In the end, this organization's blog provided a venue to spread brand messages that were authentic. Do you have a similar story? Share how your employees promoted your brand through communication channels, and join the conversation here:

http://brandfulworkforce.com/book/six-brandful-channels/
communication.

You know your communication tools are effective at promoting your brand when employees:

❑ voluntarily communicate your brand

❑ communicate your message effectively

❑ communicate your message via multiple relevant communication channels

❑ promote your brand on the job and off the job

❑ feel empowered to speak on behalf of the company openly and critically (well-intended)

❑ pull others into the conversation

❑ protect the brand when someone is bashing it, without being asked

❑ are not confused about your products, services, and mission

❑ can easily repeat key brand messages

Channel #2 for Employees to BE Brandful—CITIZENSHIP

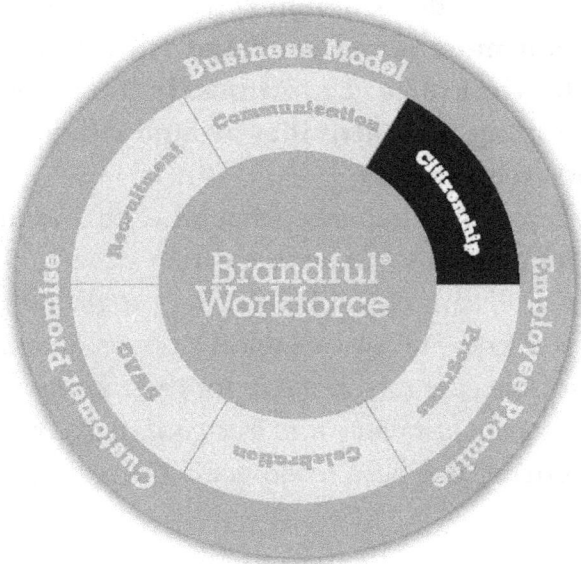

One of the often-missed opportunities in brand promotion is corporate citizenship or what I like to simply call *doing good*, which is anything an organization and its employees do benevolently to help society. *Doing good* can be corporate social responsibility programs, employee volunteerism, corporate grants, and partnerships or sponsorships with nonprofits. Sometimes *doing good* can even be spontaneous, such as the time that a JetBlue flight attendant saved a child's life—on her day off—using her CPR skills from the job.

Why is *doing good* a missed opportunity for the brand? Because the brand has not been viewed holistically as incorporating the internal essence of the organization. But now, it's taking center stage. **In fact, what organizations are on the inside equals what they are on the outside. Simultaneously, both consumers and employees want more *doing good* and it's a win-win for the brand and the workforce. Unfortunately, there are many organizations upping their activities around citizenship but not getting brand credit for it.**

There are three essential *nots*—that must be undone—to open this channel for employees to be brandful:

First, *doing good* cannot just be another program that checks a box. I know you know what I mean. It's not an integrated and a genuine part of the core raison d'être for the company. It could be perceived as *they are just doing it to look good.* If your organization needs help figuring out how to do good for real, go back to the basics section.

Second, there is no captivating mission that connects employees to citizenship. If there is no meaningful purpose for your organization to fulfill in the world (again, go back to basics, Section 1) then employees' efforts will happen in spite of your mission, not because of it.

Or third, your organization has a mission, but your employees are not connected to it. This is where you have an opportunity to demonstrate your commitment and real action—and hope they will join in. But first you must show, through your leadership, that your organization is making a true difference in the world.

Once they see progress and impact, they will want to join in. You have to build the momentum, and continually spread the progress. And let them take over when they have ideas.

Doing Good Can Attract Potential Employees and Provide Meaning.

Doing good could have a much greater impact on your brand if these programs more fully leveraged your workforce and were integrated with the brandful business basics (business model, customer and employee promise). How many recruiters actually promote the organizational social responsibility programs as part of their recruiting strategy? With the millennial generation in a quest for more meaning, and fewer out to simply make money, they are especially interested in a higher meaning in their employment opportunities. And what better way to promote your organizational brand than to have a workforce who truly believes in and yearns to participate in the citizenship programs. Find those who believe in your mission and recruit them.

Integrate Doing Good Into Your Employee Promise.

I actually hired someone who told me that a large part of her decision to join the organization was because of the tree-planting initiative that she so strongly believed in. While comparing it to her other offers, she wanted to be a part of something more than just a job, but in a place where she could get involved in a meaningful way. This shows the importance of integrating the mission, citizenship, and the employee promise. If employees don't participate in citizenship efforts, it may be that the workforce is not properly aligned with the mission or opportunities to do good.

Involve Friends and Family.

This kind of involvement is valuable promotion of your brand. When employees volunteer under your organizational name in their communities, this is powerful, sincere, and—as expressed at the beginning of this book—*genuine* marketing.

I'll share a personal story. In 2010, a tornado blew through Forest Hills, New York, which is a community in Queens, eight miles from Manhattan. (I know precisely the distance from Times Square, as I walked it following 9/11.) This is my community and was, at the time, the headquarters of JetBlue, where my office was. The tornado event had very little press and attention—who has ever heard of a tornado in New York City? But it was quite devastating for our small community. From the name—Forest Hills—you can tell that yes, we *had* plenty of trees; however, the tornado served as a natural pruning for our neighborhood. The tornado happened just as winter was approaching, so most of the rebuilding didn't start until springtime. For a few months, it was quite depressing walking to and from the train and around the neighborhood, seeing the devastation, and the constant reminder that our neighborhood had been destroyed.

And then one day while working at JetBlue, I heard the announcement. How do you think I felt when I heard JetBlue was sponsoring a tree planting in the heart of our neighborhood to restore the "forest" in Forest Hills? What a moment of hope and pride! My entire family and neighbors came out to help. My children continue to go by the park and see the trees that we personally planted, with JetBlue's support. And we watch them grow. I can say from personal experience: when families get involved, it creates an even more meaningful connection.

Ensure There Are Opportunities For Doing Good Both Locally and Globally.

Whether your organization is big or small, it's important to note that both global and local opportunities need to be accessible for *doing good*. If everything is coming out of corporate, it won't provide the type of involvement needed for everyone to be able to participate. There may be local opportunities as small and meaningful as attending Career Day at an elementary school. Tens or thousands of individual touchpoints from employees may be even more impactful than one large, more impersonal connection at the national level. Whoever your community is that you are helping, the most personal interactions are the most meaningful.

Start inside your organization with an employee foundation, where employees can help each other in time of need. The JetBlue Crewmember Crisis Fund is set up to do just this. Unexpected needs arise continually. Just because someone is employed doesn't mean he or she won't be in need of a little extra help, due to a fire, natural disaster, a death in the family, or other incident. Working in an environment where you know you have that extra support goes a long way to walking the talk. You don't always have to go to the other side of the world to encounter those in need.

Nonprofit Organizations Can Benefit.

Many outside the nonprofit world believe that nonprofits automatically *do good*. Yes, that is their mission; however, they are not all created equal. Some nonprofits have much more impact than others. Employees at nonprofits may or may not be brandful, and being brandful can have a huge impact on future funding.

Let's look at a few examples of organizations *doing good* in a way that not only makes sense to the brand, but truly makes a positive impact on others and instills pride among employees and consumers. (And I should mention that every bit of progress the organization makes from *doing good* should be celebrated—see the section on Celebrations.) Below are some examples:

Häagen-Dazs had a campaign to save the honeybee, which was integrated into their product—ice cream. They use honey in their ice cream and were able to connect the business model, customer, and employee promises together in a way with *doing good* that really propelled the company forward.

At PepsiCo, a small group of employees went to Ghana to improve water distribution. On Pepsi's website:

> **PepsiCorps** *is about more than volunteering; it speaks to the responsibilities of businesses to the communities and the larger world in which they are embedded. This theme of prospering at the intersection of what's good for business and what's good for society derives from PepsiCo's mission—Performance With Purpose.*

At Medtronic, a company that develops and manufactures innovative medical device technology and therapies to treat chronic disease, two employees were sent to Chennai, India, to research diabetes at Saveetha Medical College Hospital, a nonprofit that provides free and low-cost medical services.

TOMS Shoes is another example of a company that has leveraged a brandful workforce to advance not only their business but their cause. Every pair of shoes bought goes to buy someone in need a pair of shoes. The employees are more likely to serve as brand ambassadors when they join knowing the cause and what their participation can be.

Many organizations make small local donations, especially to schools and community organizations. It makes such a difference to the employees to know that their organization supports "me and my community." At JetBlue, pilots are encouraged to attend schools and career days to talk about their profession with youth. When a Crewmember wants to do something good in their community, JetBlue is behind them to spread the great brand.

Share how an employee has promoted a brand through citizenship:http://brandfulworkforce.com/book/six-brandful-channels/citizenship.

You know your citizenship efforts are working for your brand and not against it when:

❑ your employees are participating…and participating because they want to, not because of incentives

❑ your employees create their own citizenship opportunities

❑ you provide both local and global opportunities to get involved

❑ you provide regular updates to the entire organization with results, progress, and momentum of citizenship

❑ employees brag that the organization is helping the community, locally (and globally)

❑ employees regularly celebrate and are thankful for the citizenship contributions

❑ citizenship actions are integrated with your mission

Channel #3 for Employees to BE Brandful: EMPLOYEE
PROGRAMS

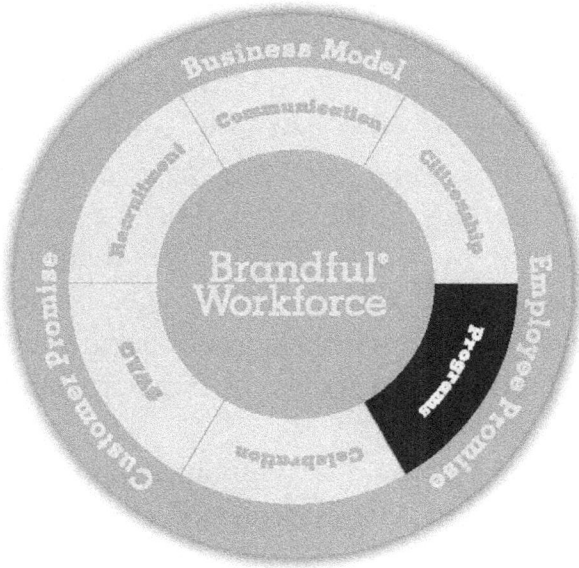

"Employee programs" deserves its own channel because these programs are not just vehicles through which employees can promote the brand, they are also *incubators in which employees can participate in shaping the evolving brand.* A key point in this book is this: *True promoters consider themselves—and in fact are—a part of what they are promoting.*

Here's a quick story about how the workforce really can be a significant part of shaping the evolving brand. At JetBlue, they regularly had meetings between the executives and frontline employees. One such meeting was with frontline employees and the head of route planning, who was discussing how they select routes and schedules. The employees at the meeting included flight attendants, pilots, mechanics, reservation agents, baggage handlers, and customer service agents. During the conversation, one employee—a customer service agent from the Lake Tahoe area—asked him why the flight at her station arrived at 11:59 p.m. instead of after midnight. He didn't seem to think that was a big deal and asked why she was asking such a question. She said, *Because the ski resorts offer a free day of skiing on the day of arrival, and a lot of our customers are missing the deal, so they are taking other airlines that arrive a few minutes later.* He was thankful for her input and I believe went back to make changes. Nobody can plan for such a great outcome for this kind of dialogue, but this really hits home on the importance of cross-functional and cross-level discussion.

To be brandful, it should go without saying that employees should be familiar with the products and services the organization delivers. The more knowledgeable employees are, the more opinionated they become. The more opinionated they are, the more they want to participate. And then some questions arise like: *How do we allow everyone to participate? Is it scalable? How do I help folks participate?*

Regardless of the many questions, there are ways to involve everyone in a meaningful way through informal and formal programs. Remember that formal programs are established by the organization, and informal programs are ones that are started by frontline employees. Both are important to building and sustaining a brandful workforce.

Let's look at some formal programs that truly get employees involved in the brand. They include: employee innovation programs, employee opinion programs, contests, and alumni programs.

Google's "20-percent time" is probably one of the most widely known employee innovation programs, in which employees can spend up to one day per week on projects about which they are most passionate. Clearly some of Google's products, such as AdSense, have been direct results of this program. However, prior to Google's program, Sony started an annual idea exposition open only to employees, to foster the exchange of ideas within departments. During the exposition, scientists and engineers display projects and interact to create a healthy climate of innovation. And more recently, LinkedIn launched [in]cubator, a program that allows a team of employees to pitch a new product idea to the executive team. If it looks promising, they can get up to three months to develop the idea further.

Employee opinion programs also get employees involved in shaping and promoting the brand. Rather than be upset when your employees are outraged over a change in your product or service, thank them for the feedback. It was actually Patagonia's employee complaints about air quality that led to their switch to organic cotton and better sustainability practices, which their brand is now known for. Employee apathy is the real enemy because they stop caring. Opinion programs usually involve committees, focus groups, or interdepartmental forums, each with a specific topic or goal. JetBlue has what they call Values Committees that gather employees from each of the major departments to help shape the brand, safety practices, internal policies, and other top-ics. Employee surveys and focus groups provide valuable insights on the brand from the employee perspective. They can weigh in on the extent they are able to deliver on customer expectations. The most impactful aspect of employee surveys is discussing the results and taking action to make the brand better, with the help of employees.

Contests are a fun way for employees as well as customers to get involved in the brand. I'll never forget the time when I lived in Ottawa, Canada, as a young teenager. There was a contest orga-nized by the *Ottawa Citizen*, our local newspaper. They hid a large amount of money somewhere in the city. Each day, they would print a clue as to where it was. At the time, I wasn't an avid news-paper reader; however, I made sure to follow the clues. The lon-ger the money went unfound, the more the suspense grew, and the more buzz was generated. It started getting television cov-erage. Groups of folks were teaming up to find the money and reexamine the clues. I would have to guess that newspaper sales grew over the course of this contest, which engaged the entire city. Finally after a few weeks, if I recall correctly, someone found the money in one of the hundreds or thousands of pipes along the Rideau Canal—which, by the way, is the longest ice-skating canal in the world. While this example may not be a contest specifically for employees, it certainly got them jazzed about the brand. And you can bet that if their friends didn't know they worked at the *Ottawa Citizen*, they did by the end of the contest.

Employee contests that are effective at building a brandful workforce get employees involved. Employees participate in nam-ing new products (*Who can come up with the best name?*), starring in an ad or in promotional materials, testing uses for a new product, and creating promotional videos and new services. Contests usually provide buzz for the communication channel.

Alumni programs can be quite powerful in providing a venue for former employees to continue to engage with the brand long after they are gone. Even though they serve other purposes, such as becoming a future recruiting source, they can be better leveraged as a pool of brand promoters. For example, General Electric and IBM both have strong alumni networks. IBM executives personally meet with alumni and value this group's thoughts and opinions. Go to their website to see more (http://www.ibm.com/ibm/greateribm). After employees leave, they can have a new perspective and offer valuable feedback to the former employer. Are you listening to your alumni?

Another potential employee program could include workplace virtual gaming that is used for training purposes, but can also be used for employees to interact with the virtual products and services. Games are developed with the idea that they will be educational and fun, and will engage employees and customers more with the brand. With 3D web upon us, there may be more interest in virtual gaming in the future.

What are some other examples of employee programs that enable employees to promote the brand? Share or view what others are sharing at http://brandfulworkforce.com/book/six-brandful-channels/employee-programs.

Now, let's look at some examples of *informal* employee programs. As we saw earlier, there is a real benefit to having grassroots or informal opportunities for employees to be brandful. Not every employee will want to participate in an official program. Having that freedom of expression can delightfully surprise you. Some employees set up their own shadowing opportunities where they can get to know other functions across the organization. These opportunities help build an understanding of the different pieces that need to come together to execute on the products or services. Shadowing also helps build meaningful connections between employees and the brand. For example at JetBlue, a pilot and a baggage handler have quite different roles; however, both impact the customer experience differently. When they shadow one another it builds mutual respect, teamwork, and better execution of the brand promise. I've seen shadowing experiences that uncovered inconsistencies or problems in processes, which could then be addressed and resolved. Those who participate in these experiences are proud of the progress they help make happen.

Sometimes employee affinity groups or clubs that are started internally can help to promote the brand. For example, some organizations have running or cycling teams. Individual employees may participate in marathons or sporting events on behalf of their organization, which supports both the employee and the brand. Sometimes clubs also focus on giving back to the community by supporting local schools and other nonprofit organizations. Ad hoc celebrations of local holidays or special events give your employees more reason to promote the brand. And finally, there seems to be a proliferation of ad hoc social media groups, crowdsourcing, and other online activities that employees are creating that can link to your brand.

Be open to your employees' activity that can boost your brand value. When employees demonstrate passion for your products and services internally, they are much more likely to be seen externally. No organization is too big or too small to get employees involved in the brand.

You know employee programs are effective at building a brandful workforce when:

❑ you don't have to pull teeth to get employees to participate. They participate enthusiastically.

❑ employees create informal programs (i.e., you can't keep up with everything they do!)

❑ employee ideas impact the evolving product/services offerings.

❑ you can continually identify specific employee contributions to your brand.

❑ customers recognize employees as a part of the brand.

Channel #4 for Employees to BE Brandful—CELEBRATION

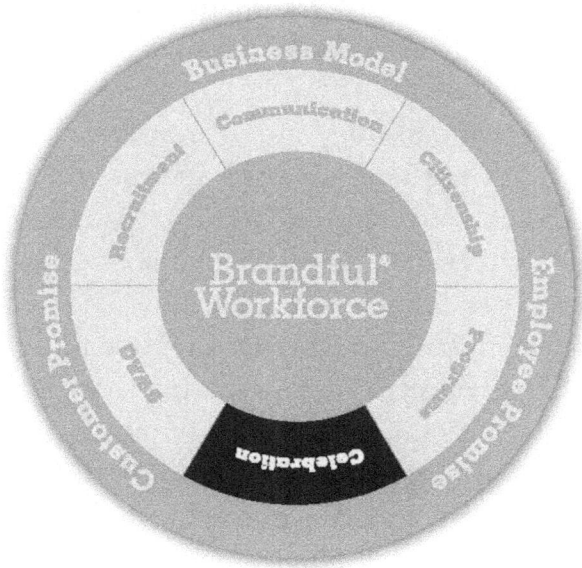

Why do many executives believe celebrating is important but don't place a priority on it? **It's a missed opportunity, particularly for the brand.**

What could be a more genuine way to promote your brand than through celebration? Celebration inherently means that you achieved something. It's progress. It's positive. **It's a way to**

spread the love of, for, and by your organization. The more you celebrate, the more often you can spread your message. On the other hand, if you're not celebrating but you are achieving something, are you not doing your organization a disservice? Are you not throwing away an opportunity? Some organizations thrive on celebrations like Wegmans and Apple. Just go to a new store launch for either company and you can feel the excitement. Lots of clapping and cheering. See Wegmans's cheer and store launch on YouTube at http://www.youtube.com/watch?v=9IKW0atrTwo &feature=youtu.be .

Warning: Don't try to integrate or introduce celebration into your culture if it's not real, organic, and genuinely wanted by your workforce. If you're trying to pump it up, begin it at the grassroots first. Otherwise, it will be fake, something that's being pushed from corporate rather than built by the workforce. If the workforce doesn't want to celebrate, you have to figure out why and address those concerns first. Resolving those issues will give reason to celebrate. Again, at this point, we are assuming that you have a successful product or service that is profitable, and there is something to celebrate. Progress and achievements are untapped opportunities to create *momentum*—more hype, buzz, and excitement from, for, and around employees.

Now that we know the answer to *why* celebration can promote the brand, let's look at five key items that employees need in order to promote the brand via celebrations.

First, employees need a culture of celebration. Nobody's going to want to celebrate if it's frowned upon or seen as a waste of time. The problem with organizations that lack a culture of celebration is they are too stressed out—either they are having trouble making profits (they don't have the money or time, which needs to be resolved before celebrating) or they are growing too quickly, which also means they don't have the time to celebrate. The other reason for not celebrating is—they just don't care; it's not a priority.

What is your organization's culture around celebrating? Is it "anything goes" and "any time"? Or is it more formalized celebrations with criteria and definitions, with everything well thought out? Or somewhere in between? Building a culture of celebration is done simultaneously top-down and bottom-up. The key is to keep the celebrations constantly aligned with the foundation described in the first section. Whatever gets celebrated should be directly associated with an achievement in the business model (i.e., profits or mission), customer promise (i.e., great reviews), and employee promise (i.e., employee achievement). This framework helps keep a shared focus on what's important to celebrate. But it's not just formally organized celebrations; employees should feel encouraged to organize on their own. When it comes from them, it automatically has a genuine nature and is more likely to be promoted. Celebration is contagious. A good celebration is one in which the folks celebrating are truly joyous about the occasion. Joy spreads naturally.

Second, to promote through celebration, employees need to know the key headline behind any celebration. Without that, they won't be able to spread and promote the message. The headline can be easily shared with friends and family in person or through social media. For example, many organizations celebrate an anniversary, but *Happy Anniversary!* is not necessarily a headline that communicates the brand, let alone promotes it. Take People's United Bank. They celebrated 170 years, and instead of just the happy anniversary sign, it said: "170 years. 0 bailouts" This sent a powerful message and was something that employees could rally behind. What is the headline of the achievement that truly speaks to the brand and gives full credit to what the organization has achieved?

It's interesting, but when you start to think about it, there could be reason to celebrate every day. With such growing fierce competition, simply remaining in existence could be a big achievement for some organizations. Do we set the threshold for an achievement too high?

Third, you may not think that your employees have the time to celebrate, but time is not as important as the *mindset* to celebrate. When I was at JetBlue, part of the meetings would include a list of accomplishments of the week, month, year—whatever was relevant. Or a weekly brown bag lunch with the team can include someone bringing in homemade cookies in celebration of an accomplishment. A celebration can be a full blown-out party—or a simple one-minute song. ***Celebrating can easily be woven into the fabric of daily work and life, if you have the right mindset.*** Some people do this naturally. Others—who tend to be nose-down in their work—need more of a mental shift. Make it a practice to go around and ask what can be celebrated. You may find a few noteworthy items.

Have you heard of a *finish line* versus a *deadline*? This is what I mean by mindset. Some folks like to just work nine to five and collect a paycheck and work up against deadlines. Others prefer to pour their heart and soul into their work; they believe in and cross the finish line with the best results possible. A finish line calls for celebration. A deadline calls for a vacation and time off. It's all in how you look at it—and why you work.

A personal side note about the celebration mindset: One of my former mentors is a great example of a leader who has a celebration mindset. On a regular basis—quarterly and annually—she would list all of the team accomplishments (big and small; personal and professional) and she would ask every member of the team to do the same. We would just go around and read off our lists of what we were proud of accomplishing that time period. We'd listen to each other. And then we would go out and celebrate—or we'd be offsite at a meeting in Las Vegas or Florida, where we could celebrate. From that experience, I began to integrate celebration into my leadership style by regularly asking my team to write down their accomplishments. Any cause for celebration, both personal and professional, we'd find a way to celebrate (a card, a potluck lunch, decorating an office or cubicle, an e-mail, a phone call, something).

Fourth, when you've achieved something noteworthy, no matter how big or how small, if you are truly proud, you will want to share it with someone. This means having the ability to invite others outside of the workplace to the organization's celebrations: your best friend, a family member, maybe not your ex-spouse... but you get the idea. When celebrations can be shared, it pulls others in—and thus spreads the brand message further. JetBlue always had venues in which employees could invite family and friends.

Fifth, employees need a fun factor if they are really going to promote the brand through celebration. At the heart of any celebration is fun. And people spread the word when it's fun. Celebrating blunders can be fun. Roasting someone special. Being playful. Including a surprise element. Got music for your celebration or for certain days? Music reminds folks to celebrate. Do you have a victory song? Mary Kay did. Need some ideas? Check online for Scott Friedman's list of fifty victory songs at www.celebrationfactor.com.

Can or should a celebration merge with an ad campaign? Has it already? What about an anniversary at a major brand like Coca-Cola? Is there a way that the employees can push the celebration to a new level? An anniversary is a good time to reflect on the brand and look back on all that has happened—ups and downs. And not just what it means to executives but to employees—some have been there a lifetime and others only joined recently. No matter their tenure, every employee probably has a heartwarming story about the organization, whether it's when they first joined, a customer interaction, or just a feeling they had while at work or while sharing their work with a friend. Do you? Share it at the following link:http://brandfulworkforce.com/book/six-brandful-channels/communication/employee-storytelling.

Sidenote:

Please do not confuse celebration with rewards or incentives. As I mentioned before, incentive programs have no role in helping to create a brandful workforce. I don't believe it can build an engaged workforce. Rewards and incentives are extrinsically motivated, whereas a brandful workforce is intrinsically motivated. If you have a well-matched workforce—one that is there for the right reasons and because they genuinely like the products, services and mission of the organization—then they don't need to be pushed or incented to behave in a desired way. They are rewarded internally when they see progress toward what matters.

For example, an international hospital based in the United States, has successfully demonstrated that an organization's culture can change favorably without incentives. While many of their peers use incentives to reinforce desired behaviors and priorities, they focus on a patients-first mission, inspiring all staff regardless of position to become caregivers. They hold everyone equally accountable and support a "no incentives" approach to building a brandful workforce.

Do you know an employee who promoted the brand through celebration? Share at http://brandfulworkforce.com/book/six-brandful-channels/celebration.

You know celebrations are effective for employees to be brandful when:

- ❑ employees own the celebrations. It's not seen as a face-time, mandatory event.

- ❑ you don't have to spend a fortune to celebrate

- ❑ celebrations happen frequently and locally as well as formally and on a big scale

- ❑ celebrations unite and do not divide.

- ❑ everyone understands the reason to celebrate

- ❑ employees can share the celebration with others

- ❑ organizational goals are clear, and when they are achieved, progress is noted

- ❑ employees feel a sense of constant progress and momentum

Channel #5 for Employees to BE Brandful—SWAG

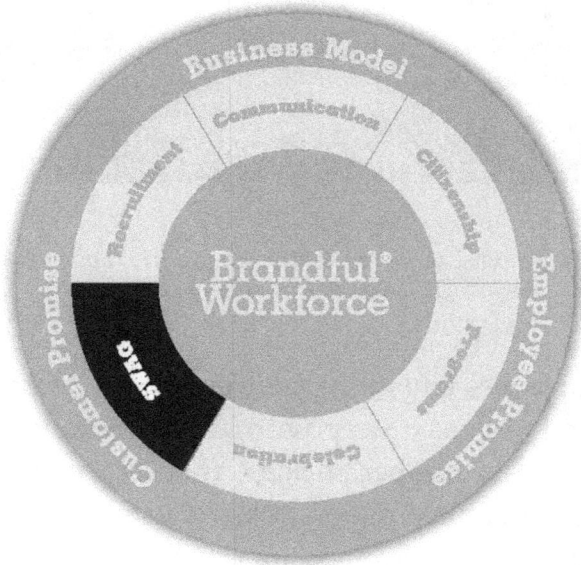

Employees can promote your brand without saying a word. There's no need to speak or shout when they can simply wear it, give it, or collect it. (or tattoo it, as shown below

"photo license terms are at http://www.flickr.com/photos/ simonov/2438326083/sizes/o/in/photostream/"

When employees truly love your brand, they want to display it, share it, and yes, even sleep with it. Swag is any item—shirts, pens, snow globes, bumper stickers, frisbees, teddy bears, hats, jackets, toys, umbrellas, pins, clocks, watches, posters, wallets, playing cards, bags, and even pajamas or slippers—that showcase the brand. Swag must have a certain cool factor and appeal. They make excellent giveaways, gifts, or collectibles.

Warning: Don't invest in swag if you haven't made it through the first section. The swag will only be thrown in the garbage or shoved in the back of a closet.

Swag is the most tangible channel for employees to be brandful, and can possibly be the most impactful on a personal level and face-to-face. Swag has the ability to touch someone and pull them into the brand. Once someone owns swag it becomes a constant reminder of the brand. Organizations used to spend millions on direct mail, to get their names and products into the households. What if employees could be a vehicle for this?

If you had a brandful workforce, isn't swag the natural extension to spreading the love for your brand?

I used to ask the marketing team at JetBlue for a bag of swag when I went on a trip, so I could have giveaways at conferences or meetings. It went far in terms of spreading the love of the organization. Who doesn't want a freebie, especially if it's cool? You can carry swag with you wherever you go, so when you spontaneously meet a customer or fellow employee, you can give it away. When there are few in supply, folks feel it's special or a collector's item. But it doesn't have to be an expensive item. It could be a button. It's the brand behind the item, not necessarily the monetary value.

Once when I was a guest on a webinar, I tried to figure out how to incorporate a giveaway online, as I was used to throwing swag into the audience. I decided to number the webinar participants and have the computer randomly generate a number—that would be the winner of swag (a bag, an umbrella, and a hat). At the end of the webinar, the host announced the winner on the call. I got an e-mail from the winner, stating how elated she was—she'd never won anything and felt like she'd won the lottery when her name was called. I sent out the swag to her and hoped she would be a loyal customer.

Voluntary use of swag by employees is empowering and pride-building. If you provide swag to employees, they will find creative ways to distribute it, and will be proud to do so. Just consider some guidelines on the distribution of your swag, keeping in mind that if there are too many obstacles and bureaucratic issues, it won't be worth the trouble for employees. Track where it goes, who's using it, and the impact your swag has on your brand.

Caution: Swag should never be a requirement to wear like a uniform. Like the other brandful channels, it's voluntary and allows employees to express their emotional connection and pride for the brand.

Swag can also be sold—how did Caterpillar start selling their boots to the public? Didn't they start out as part of the employee uniforms? And what about pilot bomber jackets? I don't know when they started selling UPS toy trucks or Oreo erasers. It's just a hunch, but I believe that there's a big untapped potential in swag—not only for employees to promote the brand, though it starts there, but much more. Consider opening up an online store for your fans—not just employees, but anyone. For example, JetBlue has ShopBlue. It's an example of how organizations can provide swag to those who are excited to promote it. Why don't more brands have items for sale that advertise their brands? It's good advertising—and it's genuine.

ShopMarriott sells Marriott beds, bath, and some decor; most likely because their customers were asking—but it's just a guess. Has Marriott considered adding more brandful products in their shop that allow fans to do more promotion? It's kind of like gift shops at tourist destinations. Restaurants sell unique T-shirts. Tourist towns—like one of my favorites, Park City, Utah—have shops that sell souvenirs. But just like tourists who want to remember their visit—and possibly return one day—loyal employees and customers want to be identified with their favorite brands—it builds their own identity. It's not just *I was there visiting*, but *I like this organization*.

Swag can also be created by the employees, for the employees, and can highlight them. Get them involved. And give it a story.

Do you know an employee who has a lot of swag and serves as a great ambassador? Share about them at http://brandfulworkforce.com/book/six-brandful-channels/swag.

You know swag is an effective channel when employees:

❑ collect it

❑ wear or display it

❑ give it out

❑ ask for it

Channel #6 for Employees to BE Brandful—RECRUITMENT

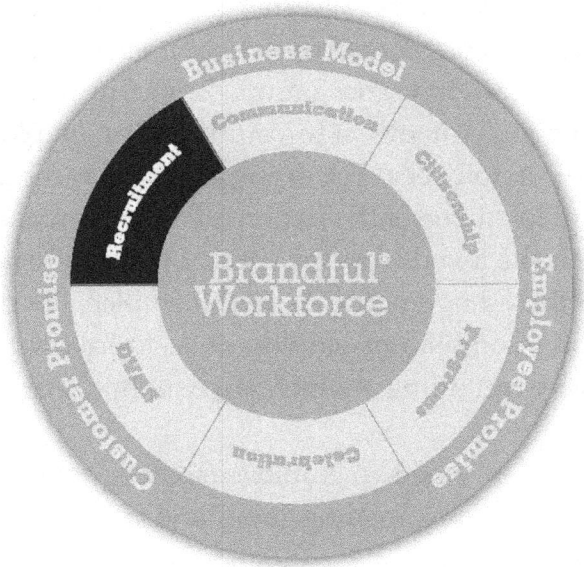

Employees are magnets for attracting new talent to the organization. When someone approaches an employee to ask about your organization as a place to work, this is an opportunity to promote the brand. Or, the scenario may be that your employees are truly brandful, and that means raving about your products and services so much so that their friends want to work there.

Either way, the act of recruiting, whether official or unofficial, can be considered as brand promotion.

Some may think that folks are desperate to find a job and employee referrals are considered as favors to the candidates. However, employees who truly love the products and services they deliver naturally want to be among others who share their passion. They tend to have a defensive mode about hiring anyone who is not a true believer—and they get upset when someone is hired who is not as passionate as they are. There's kind of a natural selection process that goes on in a brandful workforce—kind of a self-correction. You owe it to your brandful employees to hire more brandful employees. For example, I was recently speaking with a bank teller at one of the nation's leading banks and she told me how much she loved working there, but it really bothered her that some of the other employees were complacent. The best way to avoid hiring complacent employees is to involve your workforce in actively recruiting—which also can be seen as promoting your brand.

You never know when an employee may be contacted by a potential candidate. It's happening more and more. In fact, organizations are making it easier for individual employees to be found and contacted—connecting with college graduates from their alma maters or former colleagues from other organizations. Some are helping their current employees establish profiles on the company website so that others will more easily be able to find them. Others, like Unilever, encourage employees to be talent scouts, where talent scouting is part of the development plans for some of the employees. They offer online courses for effective brand ambassadors, and new hires are made aware of opportunities. Do your employees have the tools, resources, and knowledge to promote your brand to prospective employees on the hunt for a connection? These prospects may also be existing or potential customers.

You may be thinking about your employee referral program, but what I'm talking about goes beyond that. A referral program basically provides a venue for employees to point their prospects in a direction, without personally being able to help them. The recruitment channel, which provides employees an opportunity to be brandful, positions employees to personally become involved with potential candidates in a way that fosters a genuine and supportive ongoing relationship, all centered around common passion for the brand.

Empowering your employees to serve as informal recruiters gives them an extra sense of responsibility and trust, which breeds further participation, engagement, and ownership over the brand. This builds greater brand authenticity.

What should employees be encouraged to do in terms of recruiting? Below is a brief list to get your employees more involved. Keep in mind that employees already have their own established networks. In fact, some organizations are hiring folks specifically for the networks they've created.

Employees can:

- *encourage those who are brandful to apply*

- *be available to answer questions and be supportive of any candidates in their network who are brandful. When they take the time to provide information, it can boost the candidate experience.*

- *expand their network to include individuals who believe in the mission of the organization, and/or are interested in its products and services*

- *attend alma mater events or community events in their free time to represent the organization*

- *post jobs and promote the organization on their personal social media sites. Example: A recruiter at USAA posted a video of the CEO of USAA directly on his profile. Granted, he's a recruiter, but any employee with any title could do something similar.*

- *invite potential candidates for informational tours or meetings*

- *attend organized recruiting events so candidates can interact with current employees*

- *create a blog on the organization's site. For example, Rackspace, a cloud computing company, features employee blogs on their website. Check it out here: http://rackertalent.com/people/.*

- *keep in touch with folks who do not get the job, but were qualified and great candidates. This can keep them warm, should a future opening arise.*

- *be open and honest about the pros and cons of the organization and worklife. No person and no organization is perfect. Just tell it like it is.*

- *Make unique videos that show creative self-expression about the brand. See some employee-made videos from Microsoft, JetBlue, or ClearVision (http://brandfulworkforce.com).*

- *get involved in as much or little of recruiting as you want. Just be real.*

What can you do to support your employees in this role?

You need to be ready with helpful and accessible information. Whatever is made publicly available to candidates should be accessible by all employees. Materials can include: benefits, all aspects of the employee promise, job descriptions, job listings, contact with hiring managers, and guides to help them know if a candidate is a good match. Every employee should know the official recruiter for their department, job function, or team so that they can refer to them or get help.

Your goal should be to feel confident that any employee in your organization could be able to have lunch with a candidate and discuss the employee experience effectively. Having this level of confidence demonstrates a powerful brand.

Rejects Are Untapped Opportunities

What happens to all the rejects, the candidates who don't get the final job offer? If you are doing a good job at attracting the right candidates through your employee promise and brand, these folks should not go into a black hole. Are there volunteer projects, internships, focus groups, or other ways to keep these *wannabes* engaged? Why not have a category of folks who applied and want to stay in touch and get involved? Their enthusiasm and energy, if not channeled, may go to waste. This is also another way to figure out who truly is brandful. If they are that connected to your brand, they will continue to stay involved. I have heard of individuals who have stayed in touch for months, in hopes of eventually being offered a job or getting an "in." By the way, loyal customers participate voluntarily in focus groups. There's no reason why some of the candidates can't get involved. They can promote your organization by continuing to rave about the interview process, folks they met, and the entire experience. Isn't that better than turning their positive energy into a negative, which may have damaging effects?

Case-Mate, which designs cases for mobile phones, takes this quite seriously. The company is able to gain customer evangelists out of candidates, even if they don't get the job. They really take the time to establish a relationship during the candidate experience, so much so that they often stay in touch and even refer them for other jobs.

Do you know anyone who loved their job so much that they wanted their friends to become employees and customers?

Share your story at http://brandfulworkforce.com/book/
six-brandful-channels/recruitment/#axzz2dJmTREzv.

You know recruitment is effective at promoting the brand
when:

❑ the number of applications is rising

❑ the quality of hire is steady

❑ new hires promote the brand

❑ candidates promote the brand (i.e., you are getting brand
   promotion via recruitment efforts)

❑ employees want to be involved in recruiting

❑ social media has high ratings of candidate experience

Now we will turn to a new chapter on this same topic—
Recruitment. But it's seen differently. In addition to recruitment
as one of the six channels for employees to promote the brand,
we'll look at it from the organization's point of view—as a way to
build and sustain a brandful workforce.

FOUR

How To Hire Brandful Employees

The Brand GAP in Recruiting

A Brandful Recruitment Strategy Is Where Genuine Matchmaking Begins

N ow that you can build a brandful workforce from within, how do you sustain it and drive it forward? A big part of the answer can be found in brandful recruiting. To this point, we have covered: first, the brandful business basics—what your organization needs prior to building a brandful workforce; second, the six channels through which your existing employees can be brandful and promote your brand; and now we've come to the part about sustaining your brandful workforce by continually bringing in brandful employees. This section still assumes that you have completed the basics section. **Warning: If you haven't fully read and understood the Basics, please go back to that section before proceeding. If you don't have a successful**

business model, customer promise, and employee promise, you won't be able to recruit brandful employees.

Now, let's talk about taking your employee promise and *finding and hiring employees that are already brandful*, which is what brandful recruiting is all about. It is critical to be clear and transparent on who you are as an organization so that you are able to attract the right match for your brand.

The Brand Gap

Just in case you thought everything was perfect in the recruiting world, it's not. Well, it almost is, except for the gap. The brand gap is the opportunity to connect or integrate an organization's brand (not the employer brand) in the recruitment process. You might wonder how you can attract someone to work in your organization without being able to relay who you are, what you do, how you're different, what you promise to deliver, and how the new employee will be a critical part of it all. However, many organizations are currently unaware of the brand gap in their recruiting practices.

The Difference Between Traditional and Brandful Recruitment

Traditional recruitment asks: *Can the person do the specific job?* You are not building a rich brand by doing this. You are building an operation of getting the job done: producing the widget, providing the service...*but with no emotional connection.* Now there is also hiring for culture fit, which many organizations do. This may be according to the way things get done in the organization—it includes everything from communication etiquette, speed, quality of work, core values, what gets recognized and measured, etc. Still, this does not cover what *Brandful Recruitment* is all about—finding candidates with clearly established emotional ties to the brand. These folks already love, use, promote, and know the types of products and/or services provided by the organization.

Recruiting is more than just filling a skill or a head (warm body) to do the work that needs to get done. It's about growing a brand (what people think about and say about your organization behind closed doors). Every single employee is a representative of your brand and a promoter, fan, or cheerleader. They also speak out when they have constructive feedback to help the brand... they don't blindly cheer on the organization.

The Six Obstacles to Brandful Recruiting

Before I go any further, I must point out some of my pet peeves that get in the way of brandful recruiting.

One is about demonstrating that "you are the best." Many organizations say: *We attract and retain 'world class' talent* or *Look at all our awards. We are a top employer of choice.* And this is what they count on to attract good talent. Brandful recruiting is not about being the top employer of choice. What the heck does that mean, anyway? And smaller organizations are automatically left off of those lists. What? They can't be an employer of choice? Brandful recruiting is about matching the right folks with your brand—who can genuinely promote what the organization is all about.

Some of the well-known lists of top employers may be helpful but they leave out some variables that employees may be looking for as part of either the employee promise, or what's important to them in a job. Yes, it covers some of the essentials such as pay, benefits, work-life balance, diversity, and more. But it may not cover what the culture is like (organizational values like fun or integrity), alignment—whether they practice what they preach, job fit, career path, pace of change, or commuting. The lists of "best" companies also do not tell you the strength of the brand in the mind of customers, which can be a top motivator for employee engagement. How others define "best" may not always be relevant.

The second obstacle is that organizations mistakenly focus on "employer branding" as a completely separate entity from the organizational brand. There are many books on the topic of employer branding, but not this one. When you isolate your thinking about your brand as internal versus external, without considering their integration into a larger picture, you are setting yourself up for failure. Social media has broken down the walls between internal and external branding—they are, in fact, one and the same.

Thirdly, executive leadership may not set the foundation needed for brandful recruiting. The recruitment function is not responsible for creating a successful business model, customer promise, and employee promise. They simply utilize these in order to attract new employees. It's not necessarily their fault if they fail to bring in brandful employees; however, they sometimes don't have the business savvy to tell executives why they are failing and what they need. Finger pointing is all too common, especially at organizations with high leadership turnover or new leaders who have not yet proven themselves. Constant leadership change doesn't help. They create instability and change to the three pillars (business model, customer and employee promises) or the brandful workforce foundation. The average tenure of Fortune 500 CEOs is 4.6 years and declining. Organizational stability is key to keeping your promises and knowing who you are.

Fourth, recruiting is not about putting on a show. It should be real. Exposing your downsides is human. A company that learned to embrace this concept is Domino's Pizza, when two of their North Carolina employees made a disgraceful YouTube video showing some revolting pizza making. Unable to hide behind this, Domino's did the opposite. They turned a horrible episode into one that folks could rally behind and prevent in the future.

Being up front with challenges and resolving them head on seems to pay off in the eyes of employees and customers.

The fifth obstacle to brandful recruiting is attracting those you don't want. Who are you attracting? Have you ever stopped to ask: Are these the folks we want to attract? This was mentioned earlier but we'll say it again: IKEA does an excellent job at letting potential candidates know that egos will not be tolerated.

You have to ask yourself: *Why are we attracting the candidates who apply?* This is the time to reexamine your brand—how others perceive you. Perception is reality. If this does not match what you want to be, then you have some work to do.

The final obstacle to brandful recruiting: Higher salaries do not attract better quality of hire. Don't be fooled. Sure, some positions require competitive pay, but it's not a blanket statement. *The best organizations don't attract or retain employees with pay or benefits; they attract because of who they are and what they stand for—this is their authentic brand. If I'm an engineer, I can be an engineer at many different kinds of organizations— but the one I choose is the one I believe in, and hopefully the one that believes in me.* Attracting candidates through emotional connections to your brand may result in higher productivity, commitment, and retention than through salary.

How to Attract and Hire Brandful Employees

Now that I have completed the venting session above, we can move on. Here are some steps you can take in your recruitment activities to attract and hire brandful employees.

Step One: Lead recruitment efforts with your organizational brand.

Remember, at this point, your organization has already done the hard work: figuring out a great product or service that people need or want. This becomes the biggest hook for potential employees. Lead with your brand.

You can lead with your brand by recruiting folks that have an established connection to your brand or type of product or service. This can be current or potential customers, or folks that have a similar profile to your customers. Organizations such as Staples, A.C. Moore, Ann Taylor, and Kellogg's tap customers as potential employees. Or you can tap people who volunteer for a cause related to your mission, as they would already be believers in your brand.

These kinds of candidates will naturally be interested in the brand perks that you offer such as discounts, promotions, freebies, contests, special events, etc. All of this should be part of the candidate attraction. Other examples are airlines that let employees fly standby free of charge, or Apple, which provides a major discount off a limited number of products per year. Some restaurants feed their employees. Other companies provide a discount to employees and friends and family. Folks who are drawn to brand perks over salary are brandful. For example, employees at Trader Joe's say they spend their paychecks shopping there. This has your brand all over it. On the other hand, if a prospective employee is not super-excited about discounts to buy your service or product—this person may not be brandful.

How do you screen for brandfulness in the recruiting process?

Most recruiters are experienced at screening for experience, competencies, skills, and even culture fit, but being brandful? It's more or less a screen for passion for the brand. Have they used the product or service? Know anyone who did? Followed the organization on social networks, news, through friends, colleagues? What do they know or like about the product or service? Are they convincing? What kind of involvement does the candidate want to have with the brand? Will they use the perks? Are the perks important to them? Is the person demonstrating sincere passion for the mission of the organization? At JetBlue, we used to ask candidates to talk about their travel experience and favorite destinations. A common question was: *Where would you fly with the travel benefits?*

Select Brandful Candidates

Select folks who have a demonstrated passion for the products and services you provide. This means they will be interested in your brand perks. They will have opinions and ideas regarding your business, and should have experience using products or services that are similar to yours. Select candidates who are already committed to your mission and can demonstrate how it ties to their personal life.

Step Two: Integrate your online content so that it's directed to both customers and employees.

Yes, customers are the focal point for your website, but don't forget this is your front door for all potential employees. Many organizations separate career sites from the rest of the website. That's fine; however, career content can also be mixed in throughout the rest of the site. For example, there can be sidebars or notices on relevant pages such as *If you like shopping here, consider working here.* I've seen customer ads on career sites, so there's no reason it can't work the other way as well. The Container Store does a nice job at highlighting their employee stories to their customers. In a customer communication, a section was dedicated to their employees describing how their lives are impacted by the work they do. Another organization's website integrates customer and employee audiences by encouraging potential candidates on their career site to get the latest store specials by e-mail.

Step Three: Emphasize the criticality of employees to the success of the organization with specific and fresh storytelling that conveys the brand.

Some organizations show candidates detailed customer compliments of specific employees who are truly inspirational. Tom's of Maine posted an employee video that embodies their family-first values that permeates into their natural health products for families. Both customers and employees are inspired by how the company treats people. The video can be seen here: (http://www.tomsofmaine.com/video-catalog/video-detail/family-first). Others showcase individual employee values such as the $25,000 that one flight attendant's idea saved a global airline. Inspire folks to join in and be a valuable part of the organization's success. Make clear connections between great customer experience and employee dedication.

Cleveland Clinic involves every single employee in their brand, including administrators and janitors. Everyone is called a caregiver, regardless of their title. In order to improve the patient experience, which was initially believed to be determined by the doctors, they asked one patient to record every caregiver who cared for her during her five-day stay. At the end, it was clear that there were many employees other than doctors, such as nurses, phlebotomists, environmental service workers, transporters, food workers, and employees in nonclinical areas such as billing, marketing, parking, and food operations, that could have made a difference in the brand experience. Cleveland Clinic believes in a brandful workforce because any one employee can make a difference to the brand.

Step Four: Provide a genuine and respectful candidate experience that accurately reflects the employee promise and brand.

While some candidates accept offers based on the specific terms of the offer, others base it on gut instinct or what *feels* right. Create an open, safe, and informal environment in which candidates feel comfortable to be themselves. Encourage candidates to get to know the real you, and allow you to get to know them, so a good match can be made.

I was once asked by an audience of recruiters how to create an environment where candidates are not nervous and they can be themselves. It really comes down to setting an informal tone as an interviewer. You are in charge. Take a sincere interest in the candidate, what they are looking for, and their passions and experience. This way you can determine whether they are a match for your organization. Make the interview personal and professionally appropriate. Ask candidates to talk about which products or services they like best or why they like the organization. It's usually a great conversation starter and gets folks in the right frame of mind to discuss the company and job. Taking care of candidates as human beings goes a long way.

The candidate experience should reflect who you are as an organization and what you are offering in terms of the employee promise described earlier. Remember: they are trying to make a critical life decision. The more information you can provide to potential applicants, the better decision they will make…and ultimately it will be their decision, as you won't offer the job to anyone you don't want. According to a colleague of mine who works with young actors and dancers, young professionals are not fully aware of the details of a career or job before they make their career decisions. They need more exposure, or day-in-the-life programs. This will prepare new graduating classes to be brandful. An example is a friend of mine who became a veterinarian and hated it. She didn't realize that she'd have to deal equally with the pet owners (humans) as with the pets (her true love). Sometimes when young students select careers they are thinking about salary, flexibility, and the topic area, but there are different weightings given to each of these considerations. As well, there are many wild cards when you actually start working.

Allow candidates to interact with the employees, products, and services, and build the brand connection right away. Zappos, the online retailer based in Las Vegas, provides a tour of their offices and provides shuttle pickup and drop-off from the Las Vegas strip for anyone visiting the area. Other organizations can hold information sessions for potential candidates. And then there are the usual internships, mentoring programs, social media outlets, recruiting events, and public events sponsored by the organization.

What if you don't provide a genuine experience to candidates? Will they see through it? Probably, because you are an open book. My colleague was conducting a job search. She did all her research on an organization before her job interview. She astutely took notes from the website and asked questions about how they executed on their promise. She also read blogs exposing the *rants and raves,* or *dirty laundry.* There's so much information out there that your organization needs to be ready and able to answer the tough questions truthfully. Practicing what you preach is more important than ever.

First days for new employees

The first few weeks for a new employee are when they decide, and you decide, whether this is in fact a good match. The onboarding experience is just as important as the recruitment process in terms of bringing on and nurturing a brandful workforce. Intel provides new hires with dedicated greeters and gifts upon arrival as a part of their hands-on new employee orientation. This is an example of how you can welcome new hires into a brandful workforce. Orientation should include a clear familiarization of the products and services and more detail of the business model. You can't promote what you don't know. JetBlue had an airline business basics course at orientation so that all employees could understand where they fit in and how they could contribute to the success. It seems so basic, but I have been reminded that some organizations do not introduce their employees to their products. While on a family road trip, we stopped off at a fast food restaurant, one that I hadn't frequented in many years. I asked the server what was good and she immediately replied that she hadn't ever tasted anything on the menu. When I responded with a look of surprise, she continued with *Yeah, I wanted to work here because I didn't think I would like the food and wouldn't be tempted to eat it.* Need I say more?

Orientation should also include an introduction to the organization's social networks as a channel of communication and involvement. Employees can sign up as followers or fans during orientation and begin their social engagement. Employees can become familiar with the organization's Twitter account, Facebook pages, employee blogs, company internal blogs, alum networks and other forums so they are encouraged to get involved and speak up, whether it's a compliment or constructive criticism.

Constant follow-up is required to sustain a brandful recruitment process. It can ensure you are hiring the right folks and you are delivering your brand to new hires. Here are a few good signs that you are on the right track to hiring brandful employees:

New employees:

- *easily assimilate into the culture, and quickly get involved in the six brandful channels discussed earlier*

- *are able to make progress and see their individual impact on the job and on the overall organization quickly*

- *say their experience meets their expectations and is consistent with what was presented to them during the recruitment process*

What if you are not showing these positive signs? Let's round back to our original question: Will the employee promise be what's needed to successfully attract and hire the right folks to charge your organization forward and also promote the brand?

When the answer to this is *no*, here are a few considerations.

Typically, there is one or more *disconnects* that needs to be discovered. Either you are bringing in brandful employees but they are not able to integrate with your existing workforce (who may or may not be brandful), *or* your recruiting experience may not be fully integrated into the employee experience or your business model.

Do not immediately blame recruiters for not hiring brandful employees.

The recruiting arm is more of an executor of the organizational strategy. If the overall strategy is broken, the recruiting arm cannot be successful. Seen as an operational function, recruiting managers need to alert the organization to the barriers of being able to attract brandful employees. For example, recruiters should be in charge of onboarding surveys that provide insight into the new employee experience and whether it matches the intended promise. If it can't be delivered, they need to inform executive leaders to either change the promise that cannot be lived up to, or make the investments or changes so they can live up to it.

You've heard of secret shoppers? Why not have secret shoppers for the recruiting experience? How are you holding yourself accountable to the candidate experience? The promised employee experience?

Never stop assessing whether you are bringing in brandful employees. Continue to find out when and where there is malfunction, and go back to the brandful workforce road map—first phase— and look at each piece. Communication lines among recruiters and other managers across the organization need to be open and active so that ongoing adjustments can be made to your practices.

Caution! Reminder about your employee philosophy…because it's worth repeating:

If you believe anyone can do the job at your organization, and your attitude is *of course they want the job, they need the money* (assuming everyone is primarily concerned about pay), then you don't stand a chance of building a brandful workforce. You will only attract folks who simply need a job. You don't think your employees are special, and they won't think you're special. That may be fine with you and the work may get done satisfactorily. If that's what you want, the brandful workforce is not for you.

Leverage new employees to continually revitalize and freshen your brand.

New hires are the largest untapped employee assets for your brand. They provide fresh perspectives, skills, and energy, and often have the latest knowledge and information. They shouldn't just be molded into your brand, but their energy needs to be tapped and put to valuable use. For example, they can provide feedback on whether the employee promise is being delivered, and if not, they can help align it or point out the unaligned pieces. The new skills they bring in can be taught to existing employees at the same time that they learn organizational knowledge and culture.

Here's a quick tip to incorporate in your recruiting strategy. Make a list of what you want folks to say about your organization. Review prospective candidates to see if they will help portray this to your customers—and mean it—and be taken seriously like they really mean it. Determine if they are passionate about your mission. For example, anyone who works in a doctor's office should be passionate about health and exemplify this in their own lives. Employees at pet stores should own a pet. Most employees at sports stores enjoy sports. It shouldn't matter what size of organization you have, the same principle applies.

Take the Brand Gap Challenge

So, are you ready to start brandful recruiting? The following will identify if you are ready. Take sixty seconds to answer *yes* or *no* to the following questions about your organization.

- *Do you have a profitable and sustainable business model?*

- *Do you have a customer promise?*

- *Do you have an employee promise?*

- *Can you explain each of these in a compelling fashion within sixty seconds or less?*

- *Do most people in your organization know the answers consistently?*

If you answered *yes* to all the questions, then you are ready for brandful recruiting. If not, then you have some work to do. Not until you get the set of questions above answered favorably (except the last question, which can be addressed over time), should you even start to think about recruiting brandful employees.

So, are you ready to start? Do you know any organizations that do a good job of brandful recruiting? Share here: http://brandful-workforce.com/book/brandful-recruiting.

How do you know that you're on the right track?

As a leader in your organization, do you feel proud of your employees? When you walk around and interact with the employees, do you beam with pride? When you're not with employees, do you brag about them to others? If you are responding yes, then you are on the right track.

End of Brandful Recruiting: Here's what we learned:

❏ No matter how amazing a potential candidate may be in terms of skills, education, and experience, if he or she is not well matched to your organization, he or she won't be brandful. Being brandful means that you genuinely care about the organization, its purpose, products, and/or services.

❏ Employees who enter as brandful want to participate. For example, you'll see higher participation in your volunteer programs.

❏ Don't blame recruiting if the organization is not set up to allow for brandful recruiting. Complete the basics and set up your recruiting function for success.

❏ Brandful recruiting helps to create a brandful workforce, but constant assessment is necessary.

FIVE

How to Become Brandful Individually

Becoming Brandful

Here's where YOU come in

I've spent most of the book speaking to organizations on how to create a workforce that genuinely promotes the brand. Yet there's a critical audience that truly needs to be addressed if organizations really stand a chance of achieving a brandful workforce...*you*, the employee.

You can gain too—it's not just to the organization's advantage.

Why should I want to become brandful or work in a brandful workforce?

Many folks spend more time at work than they do with their loved ones. If you could make this time just as meaningful as your home life, wouldn't you be interested in at least finding out about it?

Warning: Do not proceed with learning how to become brandful if you believe:

- *work is just a paycheck*

- *fun happens only outside of work*

- *work cannot be meaningful*

- *you don't have to excel at the job to be brandful. (This book assumes that folks do their job, work hard, and perform well. If you only focus on being brandful and forget about your daily job, then you will be fired. This book simply takes the current standards and goes above them…it doesn't forget them.)*

If you know for certain that all you want is a job that allows you to pay your bills and you enjoy counting down the minutes until it's time to go home…please don't read this section. (Unless, of course, your employer bought it for you and asked you to read it. But if you bought it yourself and are currently unemployed, you may remain so, as I wouldn't want to convince you that there's a better way.)

Jobs may be hard to come by and yes, you do need to put food on the table, but to the extent possible in your life, at least look for an organization whose products and services you like, use, and/ or believe in. It will make a difference in your daily work (and life) and it will help the organization charge forward.

So, back to our question: Why should you want to become brandful?

Being brandful helps you be who you are at home and at work, 24/7. It helps you strengthen your own personal brand, live by the values that are important to you, and be engaged in the work that is most meaningful to you. It means you have found a match between your own personal brand and the brand of your employer. You'll feel more yourself, more confident and success-ful—true to who you really are. Take Mindy, a sales associate at L'Occitane. She has a passion for beauty products. Just go to the flagship store on Fifth Avenue in Manhattan and you'll see what I mean. However, it took her a while to find the right brand match, in which she could truly be herself, and love the products as well as her employer. She told me that she had worked at three other beauty retailers, and consistently left when she was lied to—or worse, she was asked to lie to customers—about what was actual-ly in the products. For Mindy, who takes her work quite seriously and passionately, like any other brandful employee, she would rather not work at all than compromise her own value system. She was head-over-heels to be at L'Occitane—at a company she truly knows, understands, believes in, and can promote.

Becoming brandful is also about the actual work and fulfill-ing a noble purpose that you believe in. It's a way to fulfill greater meaning consistently and genuinely— and connect the meaning to your daily work and the brand of your organization. Take Mr. Shapiro, a lawyer who is of retirement age; however, he confides that he never wants to retire unless he is unable to walk to work every day. He absolutely loves what he does. Compare this with someone who's in a job and counting down the days until they get to retirement and no longer need to work. They are simply putting in time, trying to simply get through it. It's a different mindset and philosophy.

Here's another mindset that conflicts with becoming brand-ful. In a news article providing career advice to college graduates, the author advises them to get a government job and not to work in private companies where there is no loyalty. He says anyone who works for a private company risks being fired—private companies are not to be trusted, as they don't value longevity anymore. He goes on to say that at least in the government, you can just do the minimum and you are guaranteed retirement and job security. According to the author, mediocrity is actually appealing because it is safe. Is this what some folks see as the future of employment?

Would you be convinced to become brandful if I told you that it makes you more competitive? When you can demonstrate your enthusiasm, interest, and knowledge in the brand, you may be more likely to be hired, promoted, or retained over others. It's a win-win for you and the organization, and many organizations are beginning to hire folks who really believe in what they are doing.

Finally, the best reason to want to become brandful is there is no extra investment needed on your part, other than to get to know who you really are, and find your brand match.

Matchmaking

It is my hope that this section will inspire you first to understand your own personal brand—who you are—and second, to take steps to find out what kind of organization truly matches your personal brand, and to learn how you can become brandful within your existing workforce or a different more suitable workforce. You need to know yourself, so you can decide what organization is a good match—including your current employer.

Sometimes I feel like a *matchmaker*. I don't make matches for love, but for work. My former boss at JetBlue used to tell Crewmembers that starting a job is like getting married and when you leave, it can be like a divorce: some are amicable and some are not. I found a lot of truth to that over the years, especially in organizations like JetBlue that build such strong emotional connections. I am passionate about helping people find their career passions—as they change over time. And this includes helping organizations to better know and explain who they are so they can provide a good and honest match to the employees. The better the match, the happier the organization and the employee will be together.

Your part is affirming that you are a true believer of the products and services that your organization delivers. And get involved to promote it. If you are not, then you need to ask yourself if you can become a believer. If you can, what can you do to become a believer? And if that doesn't work, then how can you find employment at an organization where you can be brandful?

Before we embark down the road to becoming brandful, it's important to have the right mindset.

It's Not Just About What You Do, But Where You Do It

The question *What do you want to be when you grow up?* is no longer fully relevant, as it only asks about your profession or skill but leaves out your other passions or hobbies that you discover along your life's journey. Some examples of passions are: gaming, sports, food, travel, innovation, art, writing, and entertainment. They may be the same or different from what you want to be, but can be quite relevant to your work if you choose an employer in the area of one of your passions. For example, if you choose a career as a computer technician, you have a choice regarding where you can work. Why not search for an employer in the realm of one of your passions? If you like sports, you can be a computer technician at a sports organization. Or if you like travel, you can be a computer technician in hospitality or the transportation industry.

Where you might work is not just an industry that matches your passions, but an organization whose value system resonates with yours. For example, when I chose to work at Morgan Stanley, I was specifically interested in working at a top, world-class organization. One of Morgan Stanley's values is excellence, which fit the bill. Other organizations focus on creativity or innovation, safety, teamwork, integrity, or risk-taking.

Now let's look at the steps you can take to become brandful. Being brandful starts with who you are. Then you take who you are and try to find the best match to an organization's employee promise. Once you're in a good match, being brandful will be natural. Let's look at the following sequential steps:

❑ Knowing who you are

❑ Finding your brand match

❑ Being brandful

Your Brandful Profile: Who Are You?

No two people are exactly the same—and remember, I'm speaking as an identical twin. Nobody should try to be like anyone else. The challenge is to get to know who you are, appreciate and accentuate the positive, and find an environment where you can thrive, grow—and best express yourself.

Have you ever been in a situation where you thought you knew someone and then you discovered you didn't? The same thing can happen with you. No matter how simple it may seem, it is astonishing that many folks don't know who they are or what they want. One simple way to figure this out is to answer these questions: What does a successful life look like when you are on your deathbed? What are your passions and interests? Do you have a mission? What's important to you—sports, friends, a certain cause, religion, art, entertainment, health? Where do you spend most of your time? Where do you want to spend most of your time?

Be honest with yourself.

Just as I have advised organizations to be honest with you about who they are—their products, services, purpose, and culture—I am reminding you to do the same, but about you. Be honest about your strengths and weaknesses—everybody has them, but each person comes to terms with them differently, and uses them differently. The more brutally honest you can be, the better match you will find. Do what you say. Say what you do.

There are a few items that define *Who You Are*. These are important to finding a matched organization in which you can be brandful:

- *What you're good at—skills, experience and knowledge*

- *What you like to do—outer interests and passions*

- *What defines you—personality, values, mission—your inner core*

- *What you need—benefits, pay, career path*

What You're Good At

Think about the experiences you've had in your life and what you were able to accomplish. When do those around you usually ask for your help? What is it that they ask you to do? Exploring what you are good at helps you find where you can contribute the most value. When your work is valued, you feel a sense of pride and accomplishment, and a real part of the brand. The more you are good at, the more choice you will have, and the more in demand you will be. Education, practice, and experience all help to form your solid foundation. You will need to ensure that what you're good at corresponds to the organization's job responsibilities. This is your commitment to being able to do the job well.

What you like to do

This is quite different from what you are good at, because things you like doing aren't necessarily the things you are good at, and vice versa. Questions to consider are: Where do you spend most of your time? What products and services do you use most frequently or intimately? What are your hobbies? Everyone has products and services they purchase on a regular basis like health and beauty, sports equipment, apparel, entertainment, food, financial, technology, and leisure. You can also consider products or services that you don't currently use, but would like to in the future. I often advise graduates: *If you like sports, go work in an organization that's involved in sports. If you like food, work somewhere that's in the food business.* Becoming brandful is knowing your own passions. You won't be able to be brandful at any organization unless you are genuinely passionate about the product or service you help deliver. Once you know your own passions, it will not only be genuine and authentic for you to promote a product or service that supports your true interests, but it will be a true outlet of your self-expression—who you are.

What defines you?

This is your inner being—your personality, values, and mission in life. Questions to consider are: How do you operate? What personality type are you? (There are many personality instruments that can help you figure this out.) How would you define meaningful work? Some folks want to know they are contributing to solving global or local issues such as hunger, poverty, illness, or environmental sustainability.

Yvon Chouinard, founder of Patagonia, indicates that 10 percent of his customers buy because of their shared commitment to Patagonia's way of doing business—to protect the environment. Just as customers choose products, employees can choose employers whose culture matches their inner core. As well, many organizations have certain personality types that seem to excel. For example, I was speaking with an executive from Memorial Sloan-Kettering Cancer Center, who said: *You have to be type A to be successful in this organization!*

What you need

Knowing your needs is important to defining who you are. Needs are basic necessities as well as possible deal-breakers for your job. They are the lowest common denominator of what you can accept in a job. When you look at work in this regard, your possibilities can expand or narrow, depending on how many needs you think you have. For example, I knew this one flight attendant who was an executive at a top corporation, but later in life realized that she didn't need to be paid such a high salary and wanted to travel the world. Needs are defined by the beholder and are created by other trade-offs. If you live a lavish life, then you need to have a high salary. If you live a humble life, your needs may not be as great.

Needs include items such as pay, benefits, career goals, commute time, and schedules. Finding an organization that matches your personal brand should be aligned with your needs. If you find a great organization that has everything but the commute is too far, this simple necessity can stand in the way. When you accept a job that does not meet your needs, you are making a compromise that may not last.

I spoke to Mike, a customer service representative from HomeServe, a company that provides homeowners service protection, about his needs on the job. Here's what he had to say:

Many employees take too much for granted. Too many people want to go straight to the top without just getting satisfaction from daily interactions at work. I love knowing that when I hang up the phone, I personally helped that person on the other end and provided a pleasant experience.

Consider your needs up against an organization's employee promise—what they are providing you in exchange for your work.

Finding Your Match

Employment is a choice and an agreement between two parties. Both equally depend on each other to make the right decision. Both depend on the other to be honest and up front on who they really are, so they can truly be a good match.

Now that you've considered who you are, you can move on to finding your brand match. Take a moment and think about your dream job. While working in management, I would typically ask candidates to tell me about their dream job. It was the most telling aspect of each interview. On one occasion, upon asking the question, the candidate started to cry and softly conveyed over her tears: *Nobody has ever asked me that before.* Don't wait for someone to ask you. Think about it now. And don't just consider your career or job, consider the ideal kind of organization.

Assess your current situation. If you feel you are already working in an organization that matches who you are, then you have done something right. If you're not sure whether your current employer is a good match for you, then try to connect more to your organization's brand by getting more involved and finding fellow employees who are brandful. If you surround yourself with the complainers, then you won't be able to discover what you and your organization have in common. Realizing that you're absolutely certain your current employer is not well suited to your own personal brand—or what you're all about—is also an important finding. Your work might feel fake, unvalued, or in vain. Regardless of your situation, it will behoove you to be familiar with some simple measures you can take to find your brand match. Here are a few tips for how to evaluate whether an organization may be a good match for you:

- *Connect to employees directly.*
  Putting yourself in a position to interact with employees directly can provide the most valuable information. Whether it's in person or online, you can not only get your questions answered (just be careful you speak to a range of employees as each employee will have a unique perspective), you can also gain an advantage over other candidates, as you may be able to gain an internal referral or support. Most important is how well you can integrate with current employees. Do you see similarities between yourself and the current employees?

- *Consider your own customer experience.*
  Does the product or service resonate with who you are? How does the customer experience make you feel?

- *Consult with other customers about the products and services.*
  Learn the pros and cons from the customer point of view. Do you feel motivated to address the cons and be part of the solution and be proud of the pros?

- *Investigate the senior leaders and future vision.*
  Are they inspirational and accessible? Do you believe that you can provide value to them as an employee? Are they folks that you would like to work with directly?

- *Learn what the organization has done to make a difference in the world.*
  Is the organization behaving responsibly? What are they doing that resonates with what's important to you? Can you join meaningfully in the work they are doing to make the world better?

- *Check websites, such as Career Bliss, that compile loads of helpful data on thousands of organizations.*
  This will help you be more efficient and effective in searching for your match.

Remember: Do not look for a match by searching available jobs. There doesn't need to be a job posting for you to get a job. Ask for an informational interview with anyone at any level. Once you are in, you can network within and be available should a position open up. Patience is a virtue. *Put yourself in the place of most potential.*

Once you find a great match, it takes patience and persistence to get hired. Don't give up, but continue to be open to other potential matches as well. I find that certain organizations attract many candidates and it's harder to get a job offer. Be realistic with what you have to offer. Sometimes you have to take a step down to get into the right organization where you can truly flourish. We won't explore further how to actually get hired, as there are plenty of books on that topic.

How to Be Brandful

Now you've discovered an organization that appreciates and values who you are, but how can you become involved in the brand? You can make a big difference. See how the organization can involve you and to what extent you can make a difference.

You can become brandful through the six channels of involvement that I introduced in section three: communication, citizenship, employee programs, celebration, swag, and recruitment. You already believe in the products, services, and purpose of the organization. Now all you have to do is get involved and be proactive. Organizations that truly get the brandful workforce concept *depend* on their employees to speak up—and they listen.

What you need to get involved:

- *Interest or passion—you already have that!*

- *Time outside of your regular job. I saw one organization that has a program for employees to spend a percentage of their work time helping the community; however, the employees are so swamped with deadlines on the job that they can't afford to devote any hours to the community project.*

- *Supervisor support. Your immediate supervisor must not only let you participate in brand activities, he or she must encourage it and set the example.*

- *Family support. It's easy to get carried away when you are passionate about something. The lines between personal time and work time can get blurred and it's helpful to have family and friends that understand and support what you're doing.*

- *An understanding of how you can best promote the brand. It's helpful to see ongoing examples of what other employees are doing to promote the brand. The organization should provide suggestions so that your efforts make the most impact and you're not shooting in the dark.*

- *Resources and training. Many employees are quite savvy with social media, communication, and proper etiquette—however, some are not. While you don't intend to do any harm, misunderstandings or miscommunications happen easily. Having available resources and training can be helpful to getting more involved.*

Keep in mind what it means to be brandful.

Being brandful *is*:

- *being the same person at home as you are at work. **If you have to be vastly different, then you're not being brandful.***

- *being involved meaningfully as a valued part of the brand. You believe in the product or service that you help deliver—so much so, that you are inspired to promote the brand and crush anyone found damaging it.*

Being brandful is *not*:

- *being rewarded or incented to promote the brand. It should be something you already believe in.*

- *being part of a scam or gimmick to get you to work harder for less. It's not a marketing or social media tactic. As an employee, have you been part of a recent new marketing program that attempted to get you jazzed about something that you couldn't care less about? That is the opposite of brandful.*

- *being part of false advertising. As organizations are finding it harder and harder to build authenticity, they are struggling to figure out how to effectively incorporate employees into the brand.*

Endnote

Having experienced a great brand match when I was at JetBlue. I can tell you personally how rewarding it can be and how getting involved creates more value for yourself and your employer. If you've also experienced a great brand match, please share your experience here: http://brandfulworkforce.com/book/general-discussion.

Q&A With My Readers

During the writing of this book, many questions arose from colleagues, friends, and acquaintances. Below are my answers to some of the most common questions. Following each question and answer is a link for you to continue the conversation with your question or comment.

Reader: C'mon, can employees really make or break the brand?

Julia: Of course they can. They are the ones who execute and deliver on your product or service. Look at a recent example: Anna, a receptionist at a physical rehabilitation clinic, recently greeted a new patient as she entered the clinic. The woman complained that it was too crowded. Anna said, *Ma'am, when you have a choice between going to a crowded restaurant and an empty restaurant, which one do you choose?* The client thought for a moment and said, *I get your point.* But Anna continued the conversation with *People come here because they want to get better, and they do. They get results and they tell their friends. I like that it's crowded, because that means we're doing something right.* Not only did the woman never complain again, she became a promoter of the clinic. Any single employee can impact the brand.

Ask a question or share your comment here: http://brandful-workforce.com/book/general-discussion

Reader: I believe that the work ethic of most employees is not what it used to be. Nobody joins an organization with the intent of staying more than a few years. Workforce commitment is gone and employees just want immediate gratification and advancement for mediocre work. Should organizations really care about a brandful workforce when the work ethic from the past is nowhere to be found now?

Julia: Yes. This negative mindset, while it may be true for some employees, will only lead you down a dark hole, never to emerge. You have to look at your own organization's future and determine if you have what it takes to attract and retain the right folks who will be committed, work hard, and contribute valuably to your brand. If you do, then put your trust and confidence in them.

Ask a question or share your comment here: http://brandful-workforce.com/book/general-discussion

Reader: Should employees be included in an organization's marketing and advertising strategy?

Julia: Absolutely. Individuals have more power than ever before to be able to influence the attitudes and behaviors of others—especially your customers. Even though some employees may have more influence than others, everyone has the potential to grow their level of influence. I recently came across a company that measures the influence of individual employees on the brand of their employer. The company measures the number of clicks each employee can generate when they post information about their employer's products, services, and news on their personal social networks such as LinkedIn, Twitter, Facebook, and Pinterest. Another company, Syncapse, is calculating the value of a Facebook fan for a given organization. While this work is being done for fans in general, I'd like to see what it would look like for an employee Facebook fan.

Another part of your strategy, content marketing, may provide a natural outlet for any employee who enjoys writing on topics that are of interest to your customers. Content marketing is the distribution of knowledge and wisdom in the name of your organization. As an example, Hallmark now publishes online news and media on topics of interest to their customers. What are other ways employees can be included in advertising and marketing?

Ask a question or share your comment here: http://brandful-workforce.com/book/general-discussion

Reader: OK, so you've sold me on the importance of building a brandful workforce, but how do I convince my stakeholders?

Julia: I've found that some folks instinctively get it and others don't. Many colleagues suggested I build an ROI (return on investment) model that is measurable. That's not the purpose of this book; however, it may be in future plans. The purpose of this book is simply to introduce the new thinking behind a brandful workforce. Soon, I hope to build an index that can be used for benchmarking, as a way for organizations to see where they are, and how far they have to go in terms of achieving a brandful workforce. This upcoming work could also provide further insights on costs and savings associated with a brandful workforce.

That being said—I don't believe any ROI study is necessary to convince others of the importance of this type of work, because it's common sense.

If your stakeholders don't instinctively "get" that a brandful workforce is beneficial, here are few suggestions:

- *Fear Tactic. Some CEOs respond to fear. They see someone like investment banker from Goldman, who did major damage, and they get scared that they might have an employee who could do similar harm to their brand.*

- *Rational Approach. Use data: Hey Chief, look at these numbers that support the fact that if we mobilize our employees to support our brand, it can yield us higher revenue and separate us from our competition. You would need some good data analysts, but it could be done.*

- *Concrete Approach. Provide an example that your CEO can appreciate, such as an organization like Costco, and detail how they incorporate people into the success of their business. Some folks respond well to seeing it in action.*

- *Your Turn. Insert your comments or suggestions here:* http://brandfulworkforce.com/book/general-discussion

Reader: OK. Let's say I have executive buy-in. How important are managers, below the C-Suite, in creating and sustaining a brandful workforce?

Julia: Very important. If the managers are not brandful, it can dampen the enthusiasm for the brand on the front line. As you've heard, people don't quit organizations, they quit bosses. The same goes for folks who stay and folks who are brandful—they behave this way because of their immediate role models. A brandful manager can help convert employees who are not brandful or support existing brandful behavior.

Ask a question or share your comment here: http://brandful-workforce.com/book/general-discussion

Reader: So, what are some things that a brandful leader does?

Julia: A brandful leader knows how important the team's work is to the brand and reminds them of it daily. All employees either serve customers directly, or serve others that serve the customers. A brandful leader continually makes these connections. Here are some other things a brandful leader does:

- *Facilitates work getting done. A boss is an enabler first and foremost, supporting the direct reports to get the work done successfully. He or she acts as a servant leader by breaking down the constant barriers that prevent an employee from getting the job done. The manager helps the employee to be able to succeed and pursue his or her work passion that is aligned with the business.*

- *Continually checks in with employees. The manager should also be able to see when the employee has lost the passion or is being over-challenged, bored, or checked out, and address it with the employee.*

- *Creates genuine enthusiasm for the brand because he or she is genuinely passionate about it. How do you know if a leader is really brandful? A short conversation with key questions should tell all. Like: What's your favorite product or service we offer? or What's the best part of our brand? or What are you most proud of regarding our products and/or services? Their eyes should immediately light up with excitement and enthusiasm. If not, they are not genuinely brandful.*

- *Openly and constructively criticizes the brand. A brandful boss raves about product or service offerings and points out flaws that can be improved upon—in a constructive way.*

- *Participates in the brand. The manager treats the product or service as if it's their own. They listen to constructive comments to improve the brand. They embody the values and culture of the organization in their daily lives, not just at work. They attend the citizenship events, organizational events, product launches, keep their teams informed, resolve issues, and address failures head-on and learn from them.*

- *Listens to employees. Brandful leaders ensure that the voices of their employee team are heard. The result and impact of that feedback is followed and relayed back to the employees. The impact of employee involvement is essential. When employees see that their suggestions were taken and actioned, the level of employee involvement goes up. When employee voices have no impact, their involvement goes down. When the workforce is really seen as being a critical part of the brand, management is dedicated to circling back and giving the credit where it is due.*

Ask a question or share your comment here: http://brandful-workforce.com/book/general-discussion

Reader: What kind of results should I expect from a brandful workforce?

Julia: You can expect results such as: a more competitive, interactive, and authentic brand; earned media (as opposed to paid media); higher customer loyalty; higher employee engagement; reduced turnover; increased productivity; and longer-term sustainability of your business. Here's what I mean by longer-term sustainability: Change happens constantly and the pace of change is growing so much so that some businesses become no longer viable. With a brandful workforce, you can depend on your employees to keep your business current. They provide insights that you cannot get from the customer. For example, a very low percentage of customers respond to surveys, while employees constantly get feedback that can be just as valuable.

If you think of a brandful employee as an engaged employee who genuinely loves the products and services of the organization, then the business case has already been made. There are many research reports out there that argue about the bottom-line business results of organizations with high employee engagement. There are also reports that indicate that organizations with high employee engagement outperform their peers in the market. A brandful workforce goes even beyond employee engagement, and includes not just engagement in the job, function, manager, or company mission, but passion for the actual products and services at the core of the business.

Ask a question or share your comment here: http://brandful-workforce.com/book/general-discussion

Reader: How much investment is needed to build a brandful workforce?

Julia: Very little, assuming you have a good business model that is profitable, and an integrated customer and employee promise. My advice would be to take a fraction of the advertising and marketing budget, and use it to build up your six brandful channels. Your employees may be the key to making more meaningful connections with your customers. A brandful workforce can be seen as a hidden competitive advantage, since some employees have been such strong evangelists of their brands, and may be capable of attracting and retaining customers in a way that is worth more than what you get with your advertising budget.

Ask a question or share your comment here: http://brandful-workforce.com/book/general-discussion

Reader: My organization already has a brandful workforce. What do I need to do to ensure it stays that way?

Julia: Creating a brandful workforce doesn't mean it will always be brandful.

Focus on a few key areas. One is keeping the mission alive throughout the organization—the "why," the higher purpose that everyone is dedicated to. Two is the continued alignment and transparency of the business model, customer promise, and employee promise. It's OK to change these—it's inevitable they will change—the trick is to keep them integrated as they change. And three is your people philosophy, with employees being an important part of the brand. This will ensure they continue to be meaningfully involved in the six brandful channels. Also, continue to ensure you bring in brandful employees and your leaders remain brandful.

Ask a question or share your comment here: http://brandful-workforce.com/book/general-discussion

Reader: Can any workforce become brandful?

Julia: It depends on the current state of the company and the workforce as to how long it would take. In my past conflict resolution work, every conflict had a "ripeness" level in terms of how ripe it was for resolution. I would apply the same principle to this and say that an organization needs to be "ripe" for a brandful workforce. The main challenge is having a workforce that is bitter, or opposed to management (like in unions). If conflicts between nations have been resolved, then I think it's possible for a workforce to be turned around. Of course in international reconciliation, there are changing leaders, policies, and many, many interventions that occur to create ripeness. The simplest beginning solution to creating a brandful workforce is via recruitment: to align your recruiting strategy to your brandful business basics (business model, customer promise, and employee promise)—if you are hiring.

There is also a psychological aspect behind a transformation. Referring to conflict resolution again, there is a psychological phenomenon called "good guy–bad guy." In a conflict situation, each party views the other party as a "bad guy" regardless of their actions. For example, if I hate my boss and he does something mean, like deny my request for vacation, this confirms that he's a "bad guy." But when my boss does something nice like let me leave early one day, do I believe he's a nice guy? No! According to this psychological theory, I will continue to believe he's a bad guy by believing that he has ulterior motives for letting me leave early—like maybe, he didn't want me to be around when an important client showed up. So, no matter what the scenario is, my boss will always be a "bad guy."

I'm relaying this story because the same thing happens when you try to make change in the workplace. If your employees are the opposite of brandful, and are apathetic about your brand, introducing changes to get them excited can be perceived as a trick or a ploy. The only way to combat this is through consistent, positive actions that demonstrate over and over again your message and who you are as an organization. Eventually, over time, through this consistent behavior and excellent delivery of product or service, change can occur.

Ask a question or share your comment here: http://brandful-workforce.com/book/general-discussion

Reader: In a brandful workforce, can every employee be a brand ambassador?

Julia: Yes,. Some employees will be more brandful than others. I've seen organizations designate certain employees (over others) to be brand ambassadors. They have a set of criteria and if the employee lives up to it, he is chosen. This doesn't make any sense to me. What message does this send to the employees who are not brand ambassadors? Doesn't every employee represent the brand anyway?

Employees are the biggest missed opportunity in branding today. Don't miss the boat on this one.

Ask a question or share your comment here: http://brandful-workforce.com/book/general-discussion

Reader: What happens when your top employee brand ambassador is fired?

Julia: I know this is a common fear for organizations. Anyone has the potential to do something stupid and get caught, even the star employee. I've seen it happen and it's hard to believe. Regardless of who it is or the circumstances for the termination, every employee should be treated with dignity and respect. If you are consistently caring and professional, you may be able to create some goodwill, even in the toughest situations. Terminating someone effectively and with care requires true expertise. There will always be the potential for "sour grapes," but how you handle the termination can lower your chances for damage. As well, I've found that brandful organizations will have employees stand up to those who are trying to do damage. Just keep moving forward and do what's right.

Ask a question or share your comment here: http://brandful-workforce.com/book/general-discussion

Reader: What about employees who leave voluntarily? Can you really expect them to remain brandful?

Julia: *You know you have a brandful workforce when your employees leave with broken hearts.* Employees leave for various reasons. Some leave and realize they made a mistake and end up coming back, while some leave and never look back.

Either way, they usually plan for their departure while they are still working. Your best chance of keeping your brand alive in them is to actually be supportive of their transition. This sends a message that you care about them as individuals, not just employees, and it can create a long-lasting bond. It also makes good business sense, because you want to ensure that the employees you retain are there for the right reasons—because they want to be there.

Ask a question or share your comment here: http://brandful-workforce.com/book/general-discussion

Reader: Does a brandful workforce fit different cultures?

Julia: I'll never forget the reaction I got from some French colleagues when I forwarded them a YouTube video voluntarily made by a few JetBlue employees during their personal time, about the company values. I used to speak fluent French, but cannot remember the translation for the word "hogwash"—but if I could, that is basically what they said. Why would anyone do anything work-related on their time off? That concept seemed to be almost extraterrestrial for them. But I do get that culturally, work takes on different meanings around the world, particularly with different work rules, laws, systems of government, and protections or lack thereof. Not only did these French colleagues not actually believe that an employee would do such a thing—and they did speculate that either I was lying or the JetBlue employee was lying (possibly he got paid but didn't say)—there was absolutely no space in their brains to comprehend such a thing. I started wondering if "happy employees" was an American thing. What do you think?

Ask a question or share your comment here: http://brandful-workforce.com/book/general-discussion

Reader: In a brandful workforce, you talk about the need to be transparent with employees. My organization has a lot of privacy, confidentiality, and compliance issues, which makes it tough to be completely open with employees. How do you get around this?

Julia: Be transparent about it. Tell your workforce what your constraints are and why you must work within certain boundaries, and that it's critical to the success of the business. Let them know how, when, and where to get involved in the brand. Heck, if Apple can build a brandful workforce, given all of their privacy constraints, you can! At the end of the day, every organization has to do what's best for their stakeholders; however, those that figure out how to involve employees in the brand while remaining compliant will have a competitive advantage over others.

Ask a question or share your comment here: http://brandful-workforce.com/book/general-discussion

Reader: When change happens so frequently in an organization, how do you maintain a brandful workforce?

Julia: Change is not the problem. The problem is lack of direction, or limbo, that so often accompanies change. Minimalizing the amount of time that a company is in transition and providing a clear decisive direction quickly is key. Once the new direction is set, it's reconnecting your workforce meaningfully to the changes in the products or services, in a way that they can continue to be jazzed.

Ask a question or share your comment here: http://brandful-workforce.com/book/general-discussion

Reader: Are large, global organizations at a disadvantage to smaller organizations in building and sustaining a brandful workforce? You had mentioned Lion's Choice roast beef restaurants as having much longer tenure than the typical restaurants. Is it because they are smaller?

Julia: No. Depending on your size, there are different challenges. For example, smaller companies complain about the lack of brand recognition and the difficulty of attracting and retaining employees, things that larger organizations may take for granted. I hear from larger organizations that it's tough dealing globally with a diverse workforce, and many brands—they are spread too thin. A question many of them ask is how to achieve a brandful workforce across the entire organization. Keeping it simple at the high level—the overall purpose of the organization—but different locally can serve to keep everyone united yet meaningfully connected. When employees and customers share local stories globally about the brand, this can also serve to help build a brandful workforce across regions.

Ask a new question. Click here http://brandfulworkforce.com/book/general-discussion

Conclusion

Have you ever noticed that when you purchase a product or service from someone you genuinely like, you want to go back? Any employee could be the reason that a customer purchases a product or service, over and over again, or for the very first time. Does your organization have what it takes to become brandful? Are you brandful? Send me your comments at Julia@brandful-workforce.com and let's continue the dialogue.

To write a review please send it to bookreview@brandful-workforce.com.

Acknowledgments

It seems odd to begin the acknowledgments with someone who may not even remember me from so long ago, but I thank Steven Vallevand from the hotel in Ottawa, who hired me and believed in me, and gave me the tools to be successful during the summer of 1987. That experience showed me that I could in fact find a job that I loved, where I could be appreciated and valued, that provided a desired service loved by the customers. As a concierge, I truly felt that I was welcoming visitors from all over the world to the capitol of Canada and sharing my love for the city of Ottawa with them. Because of this early experience, I had the confidence to continue to follow my passions throughtout my career.

Below is a 1987 newspaper clipping of two brandful employees.

It was really my parents who first encouraged me to follow my passions. As the daughter of a rabbi, it was natural for me to want meaning and purpose in my work. It was my grandmother (born in 1916) and mother who both worked hard in their careers, and served as female role models to me on how to integrate work and home, successfully. My husband, a self-made man and entrepreneur, provides the business savvy, common sense and love to support my work.

Hotel redoubles effort to attract more tourists

By Sol Chrom
Citizen staff writer

Visitors to the downtown Holiday Inn at Queen and Kent Streets might be forgiven for doing a double take if they walk into the lobby at the right time of day.

They'll more than likely be greeted with a friendly smile from an attractive, brightly-dressed young blonde woman.

A bit farther along and they'll be greeted with an equally-friendly smile from an equally-brightly dressed blonde young woman — who looks just like the first one.

The two are identical twins who have talked their way into a pair of highly-visible positions, greeting and guiding the hotel's guests during their stay in the nation's capital.

Janet and Julie Marcus, both 17, are the most visible part of the hotel's effort to spruce up its tourist package.

"Their end is the hardest thing to do," says front office manager Steven Vallevand. "They really have to push the business, and show what tourists can do in Ottawa."

Julie, a Grade 11 student at Sir Robert Borden High School in Nepean, wants to go into hotel management. She and Janet decided to apply separately after a joint interview at the Roxborough Hotel didn't work out.

"We figured we should go separately because we were both talking at the same time."

Both applied at the Holiday Inn, although Janet's application came as an afterthought to Julie's.

"They both applied just about the same time we decided to set up the summer package and hire somebody," says Vallevand. "The personnel office told me it just happened to have two terrific girls — I've never seen anyone arrive so fast for an interview."

Julie says the best thing about the job, which pays $4.50 an hour, is meeting people.

Julie Marcus, left, and her identical twin Janet take double-barrelled aim at attracting tourist trade

"My identical twin sister, Janet, and me, being brandful."

Thanks to my parents, Rabbi Sandy and Ruth Marcus, and my sister and brother, Janet Marcus and Jonathan Marcus. Thanks to Diofanor, Rosalba, and Anamaria Gomez.

Thanks to Irene Calvin, Danielle Bencivenga, and Stephanie Hansen, who worked with me at JetBlue Airways and helped formulate the original concept behind a brandful workforce. Thanks to David Neeleman, founder of JetBlue, for creating a company built by a brandful workforce, and for Vinny Stabile and Barbara Shea for sustaining it and embracing me in the brandful workforce when I arrived. Thanks to Tara Di Domenico, Jason Feliciano,

Jeremy Kasle, Peng Lim, and Wendy Petties, the best team anyone could have led. They probably taught me more than I taught
them. Thanks to John Hollon and Marlene Lipson who helped
edit. Thanks to my graphic designers, Alison Crawford and
Evan Ginsberg, and my video artists, Todd Smith and Catharine
Fennell. Thanks to many others who understand the value of a
brandful workforce and support this work: Ze McFarland, Bill
Sinunu, Brian Hackett, Max Kalehoff and Susan LaMotte.

And to all those who are brandful or want to become brandful: you have inspired me to write this book.